T0255164

SpringerBriefs in Computer Science

SpringerBriefs present concise summaries of cutting-edge research and practical applications across a wide spectrum of fields. Featuring compact volumes of 50 to 125 pages, the series covers a range of content from professional to academic.

Typical topics might include:

- A timely report of state-of-the art analytical techniques
- A bridge between new research results, as published in journal articles, and a contextual literature review
- A snapshot of a hot or emerging topic
- An in-depth case study or clinical example
- A presentation of core concepts that students must understand in order to make independent contributions

Briefs allow authors to present their ideas and readers to absorb them with minimal time investment. Briefs will be published as part of Springer's eBook collection, with millions of users worldwide. In addition, Briefs will be available for individual print and electronic purchase. Briefs are characterized by fast, global electronic dissemination, standard publishing contracts, easy-to-use manuscript preparation and formatting guidelines, and expedited production schedules. We aim for publication 8–12 weeks after acceptance. Both solicited and unsolicited manuscripts are considered for publication in this series.

**Indexing: This series is indexed in Scopus, Ei-Compendex, and zbMATH **

More information about this series at https://link.springer.com/bookseries/10028

Balázs Pejó · Damien Desfontaines

Guide to Differential Privacy Modifications

A Taxonomy of Variants and Extensions

Balázs Pejó
Department of Networked Systems
and Services
Budapest University of Technology
and Economics
Budapest, Hungary

Damien Desfontaines
Tumult Labs
Zurich, Switzerland

ISSN 2191-5768   ISSN 2191-5776 (electronic)
SpringerBriefs in Computer Science
ISBN 978-3-030-96397-2   ISBN 978-3-030-96398-9 (eBook)
https://doi.org/10.1007/978-3-030-96398-9

This Springer imprint is published by the registered company Springer Nature Switzerland AG
The registered company address is: Gewerbestrasse 11, 6330 Cham, Switzerland

Preface

Shortly after it was first introduced in 2006, differential privacy became the flagship data privacy definition. Since then, numerous variants and extensions were proposed to adapt it to different scenarios and attacker models. In this book, we propose a systematic guide for these modifications. We list all data privacy definitions based on differential privacy and partition them into seven categories, depending on which aspect of the original definition is modified.

These categories act like dimensions: Usually, modifications from the same category cannot be combined, but modifications from different categories can be combined to form new definitions. We also establish a partial ordering of relative strength between these notions by summarizing existing results. Furthermore, we list which of these definitions satisfy some desirable properties, like composition, post-processing, and convexity by either providing a novel proof or collecting existing ones.

We hope this seminal work makes it easier for new practitioners to understand whether their use case needs an alternative differential privacy definition, and if so, which existing notions are the most appropriate and what their basic properties are.

Budapest, Hungary
Zurich, Switzerland

Balázs Pejó
Damien Desfontaines

Contents

Chapter 1
Introduction

What does it mean for data to be anonymized? It was discovered that removing explicit identifiers from dataset records was not enough to prevent information from being re-identified [1, 2], and they proposed the first definition of anonymization. This notion, called *k-anonymity*, is a property of a dataset: Each combination of re-identifying fields must be present at least k times. In the following decade, further research showed that sensitive information about individuals could still be leaked when releasing k-anonymous datasets, and many variants and definitions were proposed, such as *l-diversity* [3], *t-closeness* [4], *n-confusion* [5], and so on.

A common shortcoming of these approaches is that they defined anonymity as a property of the dataset: Without knowing how the dataset is generated, arbitrary information can be leaked. This approach was changed with the introduction of *differential privacy* (DP) [6, 7]: rather than being a property of the sanitized dataset, anonymity was instead defined as a property of the process. It was inspired by Dalenius' privacy goal that "Anything about an individual that can be learned from the dataset can also be learned without access to the dataset" [8], a goal similar to one already used in probabilistic encryption [9].

Thanks to its useful properties, DP quickly became the flagship of data privacy definitions. Many algorithms and statistical processes were changed to satisfy DP and were adopted by organizations like Apple [10], Facebook [11, 12], Google [13–16], LinkedIn [17, 18], Microsoft [19], and the US Census Bureau [20] [21] [22].

Since the original introduction of DP, many modifications have been proposed to adapt it to different contexts or assumptions. These new definitions enable practitioners to get privacy guarantees, even in cases that the original DP definition does not cover well. This happens in a variety of scenarios: The noise mandated by DP can be too large and force the data custodian to consider a weaker alternative, the risk model might be inappropriate for certain use cases, or the context might require the data owner to make stronger statements on what information the privacy mechanism can reveal.

B. Pejó and D. Desfontaines, *Guide to Differential Privacy Modifications*,
SpringerBriefs in Computer Science,
https://doi.org/10.1007/978-3-030-96398-9_1

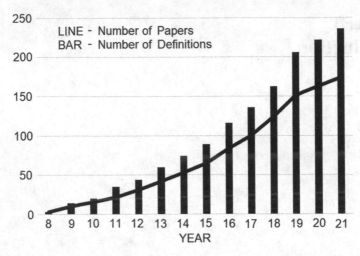

Fig. 1.1 Accumulated number of papers which are introducing new DP notions (line) and the exact number of these definitions (bar) for the years from 2008 till 2021.

Figure 1.1 shows the prevalence of this phenomenon: The number of papers proposing new modifications is increasing. We visualize all papers and definitions which presented a DP modifications as new. Currently, there are approximately *200* semantically different notions inspired by DP, which were defined in the last 16 years. These can be "extensions" or "variants" of DP. An extension encompasses the original DP notion as a special case, while a variant changes some aspect, typically to weaken or strengthen the original definition.

With so many definitions, it is difficult for new practitioners to get an overview of this research area. Many definitions have similar goals, so it is also challenging to understand which are appropriate to use in which context. These difficulties also affect experts: A number of definitions listed in this work have been defined independently multiple times (often with identical semantic meaning but different names or identical names but different semantic meanings). Finally, they are often introduced without a comparison to related notions.

This book attempts to solve these problems. It is a systematization of knowledge and a taxonomy of modifications of DP, providing short explanations of the intuition, use cases, and basic properties of each. By categorizing these definitions, we attempt to simplify the understanding of existing variants and extensions, and of the relations between them. We hope to make it easier for new practitioners to understand whether their use case needs an alternative definition, and if so, which existing notions are the most appropriate and what their basic properties are.

Organization

We systematize the scientific literature on modifications of DP and propose a unified and comprehensive taxonomy of these definitions by proposing seven "dimensions." These are ways in which the original definition of DP can be modified or extended. We list variants and extensions that belong to each dimension, and we highlight representative definitions for each. Whenever possible, we compare these definitions and establish a partial ordering between the strengths of different notions. Furthermore, for each definition, we specify whether it satisfies the privacy axioms (post-processing and convexity) [23, 24], and whether they are composable.

Our book is organized as follows:

- In Chap. 2, we recall the original definition of DP and introduce our dimensions along which DP can be modified. Moreover, we present the basic properties of DP and define how definitions can relate to each other.
- In the following seven chapters (Chaps. 3–9), we introduce our dimensions and list and compare the corresponding definitions.
- In Chap. 10, we summarize the results from the previous chapters into tables, showing the corresponding properties with reference to the proofs and list the known relations.
- In Chap. 11, we detail the methodology and scope of this book and review the related literature.
- Finally, in Chap. 12, we conclude this book.

References

1. Samarati, P.: Protecting respondents identities in microdata release. IEEE Trans. Knowl. Data Eng. (2001)
2. Sweeney, L.: k-anonymity: a model for protecting privacy. Int. J. Uncertainty, Fuzziness Knowl. Based Syst. (2002)
3. Machanavajjhala, A., Gehrke, J., Kifer, D., Venkitasubramaniam, M.: l-diversity: privacy beyond k-anonymity. In: Proceedings of the 22nd International Conference on Data Engineering, 2006. ICDE'06. IEEE (2006)
4. Li, N., Li, T., Venkatasubramanian, S.: t-closeness: privacy beyond k-anonymity and l-diversity. In: IEEE 23rd International Conference on Data Engineering, 2007. ICDE 2007. IEEE (2007)
5. Stokes, K., Torra, V.: n-confusion: a generalization of k-anonymity. In: Proceedings of the 2012 Joint EDBT/ICDT Workshops. ACM (2012)
6. Dwork, C., McSherry, F.: Differential data privacy (2005)
7. Dwork, C.: Differential privacy. In: Proceedings of the 33rd international conference on Automata, Languages and Programming. ACM (2006)
8. Dalenius, T.: Towards a methodology for statistical disclosure control. statistik Tidskrift (1977)
9. Shafi, G., Micali, S.: Probabilistic encryption. J. Comput. Syst. Sci. (1984)
10. Differential Privacy Team: Learning with privacy at scale. https://machinelearning.apple.com/docs/learning-with-privacy-at-scale/appledifferentialprivacysystem.pdf (2017)
11. Messing, S., DeGregorio, C., Hillenbrand, B., King, G., Mahanti, S., Mukerjee, Z., Nayak, C., State, B., Wilkins, A.: Facebook Privacy-Protected Full URLs Data Set, Nate Persily (2020)
12. Herdağdelen, A., Dow, A., State, B., Mohassel, P., Pompe, A.: Protecting privacy in facebook mobility data during the covid-19 response (2020). https://research.fb.com/blog/2020/06/protecting-privacy-in-facebook-mobility-data-during-the-covid-19-response/
13. Aktay, A., Bavadekar, S., Cossoul, G., Davis, J., Desfontaines, D., Fabrikant, A., Gabrilovich, E., Gadepalli, K., Gipson, B., Guevara, M., Kamath, C., Kansal, M., Lange, A., Mandayam,

C., Oplinger, A., Pluntke, C., Roessler, T., Schlosberg, A., Shekel, T., Vispute, S., Vu, M., Wellenius, G., Williams, B., Wilson, R.J.: Google covid-19 community mobility reports: anonymization process description (version 1.1) (2020)

14. Bavadekar, S., Dai, A., Davis, J., Desfontaines, D., Eckstein, I., Everett, K., Fabrikant, A., Flores, G., Gabrilovich, E., Gadepalli, K., Glass, S., Huang, R., Kamath, C., Kraft, D., Kumok, A., Marfatia, H., Mayer, Y., Miller, B., Pearce, A., Perera, I.M., Ramachandran, V., Raman, K., Roessler, T., Shafran, I., Shekel, T., Stanton, C., Stimes, J., Sun, M., Wellenius, G., Zoghi, M.: Google covid-19 search trends symptoms dataset: anonymization process description (version 1.0) (2020)

15. Bavadekar, S., Boulanger, A., Davis, J., Desfontaines, D., Gabrilovich, E., Gadepalli, K., Ghazi, B., Griffith, T., Gupta, J., Kamath, C., Kraft, D., Kumar, R., Kumok, A., Mayer, Y., Manurangsi, P., Patankar, A., Perera, I.M., Scott, C., Shekel, T., Miller, B., Smith, K., Stanton, C., Sun, M., Young, M., Wellenius, G.: Google covid-19 vaccination search insights: anonymization process description (2021)

16. Wilson, R.J., Zhang, C.Y., Lam, W., Desfontaines, D., Marengo, D.S., Gipson, B.: Differentially private sql with bounded user contribution. Proceedings on Privacy Enhancing Technologies, vol. 2, pp. 230–250 (2020)

17. Rogers, R., Cardoso, A.R., Mancuhan, K., Kaura, A., Gahlawat, N., Jain, N., Ko, P., Ahammad, P.: A members first approach to enabling linkedin's labor market insights at scale (2020)

18. Rogers, R., Subramaniam, S., Peng, S., Durfee, D., Lee, S., Kancha, S.K., Sahay, S., Ahammad, P.: A privacy preserving data analytics system at scale. Linkedin's audience engagements api (2020)

19. Ding, B., Kulkarni, J., Yekhanin, S.: Collecting telemetry data privately. In: Advances in Neural Information Processing Systems (2017)

20. Abowd, J.M., Andersson, F., Graham, M., Vilhuber, L., Wu, J.: Formal privacy guarantees and analytical validity of on the map public-use data. https://ecommons.cornell.edu/handle/1813/47672 (2010)

21. Garfinkel, S.L., Abowd, J.M., Powazek, S.: Issues encountered deploying differential privacy. In: Proceedings of the 2018 Workshop on Privacy in the Electronic Society. ACM (2018)

22. Foote, A.D., Machanavajjhala, A., McKinney, K.: Releasing earnings distributions using differential privacy: disclosure avoidance system for post-secondary employment outcomes (PSEO). J. Privacy Confidentiality 9(2) (2019)

23. Kifer, D., Lin, B.-R.: Towards an axiomatization of statistical privacy and utility. In: Proceedings of the twenty-ninth ACM SIGMOD-SIGACT-SIGART symposium on Principles of database systems. ACM (2010)

24. Kifer, D., Lin, B.-R.: An axiomatic view of statistical privacy and utility. J. Privacy Confidentiality (2012)

Chapter 2
Differential Privacy

In this chapter, we recap the original DP definition with its basic properties, define how definitions can related to each other, and introduce our dimensions along which DP can be modified.

Let $\mathcal{T}$ denote an arbitrary set of possible records. We typically use t to denote the records themselves. A dataset is a finite indexed family of records. We denote by $\mathcal{D}$ space of possible datasets, and individuals datasets are typically called D, D', D_1 or D_2. The indices of a dataset are typically called i and j, with $D(i)$ referring to the ith record of a dataset D. We denote by D_{-i} the dataset D whose ith record has been removed.

Let $\mathcal{O}$ denote the set of possible outputs; outputs are typically called O, and sets of an arbitrary outputs are called S. A mechanism is a randomized function which takes a dataset as input and returns an output. Mechanisms are typically called $\mathcal{M}$, while $\mathcal{M}(D)$ is usually a random variable. Probability distributions on $\mathcal{T}$ are called π, probability distributions on $\mathcal{D}$ are called θ, and family of probability distributions on $\mathcal{T}$ and on $\mathcal{D}$ is called Π and Θ, respectively. Table 2.1 summarizes these notations, while others will be detailed later (i.e., when used) in the book.

2.1 The Original Version

The first DP mechanism, randomized response, was proposed in 1965 [1], and data privacy definitions that are a property of a mechanism and not of the output dataset were already proposed in as early as 2003 [2]. However, DP and the related notion of ε-*indistinguishability* were first formally defined in 2006 [3–5].

© The Author(s), under exclusive license to Springer Nature Switzerland AG 2022
B. Pejó and D. Desfontaines, *Guide to Differential Privacy Modifications*,
SpringerBriefs in Computer Science,
https://doi.org/10.1007/978-3-030-96398-9_2

Table 2.1 Notations used in this book

Notation	Description
$t \in \mathcal{T}$	A possible record and the set of possible records
$\mathcal{D} = \mathcal{T}^*$	Set of possible datasets (sequences of records)
$D \in \mathcal{D}$	Dataset (we also use D', D_1, D_2, ...)
$D(i)$	ith record of the dataset ($i \le |D|$)
D_{-i}	Dataset D, with its ith record removed
$S \subseteq \mathcal{O}$	Subset of possible outputs and the set of possible outputs
$O \in \mathcal{O}$	Output of the privacy mechanism
$\mathcal{M} : \mathcal{D} \to \mathcal{O}$	Privacy mechanism (probabilistic)
$\mathcal{M}(D)$	The distribution (or an instance thereof) of the outputs of $\mathcal{M}$ given input D
$d_{\mathcal{D}}$	Distance function between datasets
$\phi \in \Phi$	(Family of) sensitive predicates on datasets ($\phi \subseteq \mathcal{D}$)
$\pi \in \Pi$	(Family of) probability distributions on $\mathcal{T}$
$B \in \mathcal{B}$	(Family of) possible background knowledge (we also use $\hat{B}$)
$\theta \in \Theta$	(Family of) probability distribution on $\mathcal{D}$, on $\mathcal{D} \times \mathcal{B}$
$\mathcal{M}(D)_{|D \sim \theta, \phi}$	Distribution of outputs of $\mathcal{M}$ given an input drawn from θ, conditioned on ϕ
Ω	Probabilistic polynomial-time Turing machine, called distinguisher

Definition 2.1 (ε-*indistinguishability* [5]). Two random variables A and B are ε-indistinguishable, denoted $A \approx_\varepsilon B$, if for all measurable sets X of possible events:

$$\mathbb{P}[A \in X] \le e^\varepsilon \cdot \mathbb{P}[B \in X] \quad \text{and} \quad \mathbb{P}[B \in X] \le e^\varepsilon \cdot \mathbb{P}[A \in X]$$

Informally, A and B are ε-indistinguishable if their distributions are "close." This notion originates from the cryptographic notion of indistinguishability [6]. A similar notion, $(1, \varepsilon)$-*privacy*, was defined in [7], where $(1 + \varepsilon)$ used in place of e^ε, and it was also called *log-ratio distance* in [8].

The notion of ε-indistinguishability is then used to define DP.

Definition 2.2 (ε-*differential privacy* [4]). A privacy mechanism $\mathcal{M}$ is ε-differential private (or ε-DP) if for all datasets D_1 and D_2 that differ only in one record, $\mathcal{M}(D_1) \approx_\varepsilon \mathcal{M}(D_2)$.

Mechanisms

Besides the random response mechanism (which returns the true value with probability p and returns a random value otherwise), in general there are three places where noise can be injected to guarantee DP [9]: It can be added to the input, to the output, and directly to the mechanism. For instance, in machine learning, context input (e.g., [10]) and output (e.g., [11]) perturbation are equivalent with sanitizing the dataset before and the predictions after the training, respectively. Concerning mechanism perturbation, there are various techniques, such as loss function perturbation (e.g.,

[12]) and gradient perturbation (e.g., [13]), which insert noise to the model objective and update, respectively.

The most widely used distributions the noise is sampled from are Laplace, Gauss, and exponential. Using the first and last makes any underlying mechanism to satisfy ε-DP for continuous and discrete cases; however, they could result in large added noise. On the contrary, the middle distribution decreases the probability of such events significantly, but the obtained differential privacy guarantee is weaker (i.e., (ε, δ)-DP, introduced in Sect. 3.

2.2 Dimensions

Novel DP definitions modify the original definition in various ways. To establish a comprehensive taxonomy, a natural approach is to partition them into "categories," depending on which aspect of the definition they change. Unfortunately, this approach fails for privacy definitions, many of which modify several aspects at once, so it is impossible to have a categorization such that every definition falls neatly into only one category.

We utilize the notion "dimensions" to capture the various ideas how the original DP definition could be changed. Each variant or extension of DP can be seen as a point in a multidimensional space, where each axis corresponds to one possible way of changing the definition along a particular dimension. To make this representation possible, our dimensions need to satisfy two properties:

1. **Mutual compatibility**: definitions that vary along different dimensions can be combined to form a new, meaningful definition.
2. **Inner exclusivity**: definitions in the same dimension cannot be combined to form a new, meaningful definition (but they can be pairwise comparable).

Although the first point is satisfied by our dimension-based systematization, the second does not hold for several definitions corresponding to some dimensions. This is because we capture "ideas" with the dimensions, which might be achieved in multiple ways. By dividing further these dimensions, we could have obtain a more fine-grained systematization, yet that would result in many separate but intertwined dimensions. Instead, we defined seven clear and easily motivatable dimensions, with intuitive explanation of what it means to modify DP along each dimension. Moreover, each possible choice within a dimension should be similarly understandable, to allow new practitioners to determine quickly which kind of definition they should use or study, depending on their use case.

We introduce our dimensions by reformulating the guarantee offered by DP and highlight aspects that have been modified. Each dimension is attributed a letter, and we note the dimension letter corresponding to each highlight. This formulation considers the point of view of an attacker, trying to find out some sensitive information about some input data using the output of a mechanism.

Table 2.2 Seven dimensions and their typical motivation

Dimension	Description	Typical motivations
Q uantification of privacy loss	How is the privacy loss quantified across outputs?	Averaging risk, obtaining better composition properties
N eighborhood Definition	Which properties are protected from the attacker?	Protecting specific values or multiple individuals
V ariation of Privacy Loss	Can the privacy loss vary across inputs?	Modeling users with different privacy requirements
B ackground Knowledge	How much prior knowledge does the attacker have?	Using mechanisms that add less or no noise to data
F ormalism change	Which formalism is used to describe the attacker's knowledge gain?	Exploring other intuitive notions of privacy
R elativization of Knowledge Gain	What is the knowledge gain relative to?	Guaranteeing privacy for correlated data
C omputational power	How much computational power can the attacker use?	Combining cryptography techniques with DP

An attacker with **perfect background knowledge** (B) and **unbounded computation power** (C) is **unable** (R) to **distinguish** (F) **anything about an individual** (N), **uniformly across users** (V) even in the **worst-case scenario** (Q).

This informal definition of DP with the seven highlighted aspects give us seven distinct dimensions. We denote each one by a letter and summarize them in Table 2.2. Each is introduced in its corresponding chapter.

Note that the interpretation of DP is subject to some debate. In [14], authors summarize this debate and show that DP can be interpreted under two possible lenses: It can be seen as an "associative" property, or as a "causal" property. The difference between the two interpretations is particularly clear when one supposes that the input dataset is modeled as being generated by a probability distribution.

- In the associative view, this probability distribution is conditioned upon the value of one record. If the distribution has correlations, this change can affect other records as well.
- In the causal view, the dataset is first generated, and the value of one record is then changed before computing the result of the mechanism.

While the causal view does not require any additional assumption to capture the intuition behind DP, the associative view requires that either all records are independent in the original probability distribution (the "independence assumption"), or the adversary must know all data points except one (the "strong adversary assumption", which we picked in the reformulation above).

These considerations can have a significant impact on DP modifications, leading either to distinct variants that attempt to capture the same intuition or to the same variant being interpreted in different ways.

2.3 Properties

Privacy Axioms

Two important properties of data privacy notions are called privacy axioms, proposed in [15, 16]. These are not axioms in a sense that they assumed to be true; rather, they are consistency checks: Properties that, if not satisfied by a data privacy definition, indicate a flaw in the definition[1].

Definition 2.3 (*Privacy axioms* [15, 16]).

- **Post-processing** (or "transformation invariance"): A privacy definition Def satisfies the post-processing axiom if, for any mechanism $\mathcal{M}$ satisfying Def and any probabilistic function f, the mechanism $D \to f(\mathcal{M}(D))$ also satisfies Def.
- **Convexity** (or "privacy axiom of choice"): A privacy definition Def satisfies the convexity axiom if, for any two mechanisms $\mathcal{M}_1$ and $\mathcal{M}_2$ satisfying Def, the mechanism $\mathcal{M}$ defined by $\mathcal{M}(D) = \mathcal{M}_1(D)$ with probability p and $\mathcal{M}(D) = \mathcal{M}_2(D)$ with probability $1 - p$ also satisfies Def.

Composition

A third important property is one of DP's main strengths: composability. It guarantees that the output of two mechanisms satisfying a privacy definition still satisfies the definition, typically with a change in parameters. There are several types of composition: parallel composition, sequential composition, and adaptive composition. We introduce the first two below.

Theorem (Parallel composition [4]). *Let $\mathcal{M}_1$ be a ε_1-DP mechanism, and $\mathcal{M}_2$ a ε_2-DP mechanism. For any dataset D, let D_1 and D_2 be the result of an operation that separates records in two disjoint datasets. Then, the mechanism $\mathcal{M}$ defined by $\mathcal{M}(D) = (\mathcal{M}_1(D_1), \mathcal{M}_2(D_2))$ is $\max(\varepsilon_1, \varepsilon_2)$-DP.*

Paralel composition allows us to build "locally" differentially private mechanisms (more detail in Chap. 11), in which a central server can compute global statistics without accessing the raw data from each user.

Theorem (*Sequential composition [4]*). *Let $\mathcal{M}_1$ be a ε_1-DP mechanism, and $\mathcal{M}_2$ a ε_2-DP mechanism. Then, the mechanism $\mathcal{M}$ defined by $\mathcal{M}(D) = (\mathcal{M}_1(D), \mathcal{M}_2(D))$ is $(\varepsilon_1 + \varepsilon_2)$-DP.*

Moreover, the composition of adaptive, if this theorem stays true when $\mathcal{M}_2$ depends on the value of $\mathcal{M}_1(D)$. This latter property allows to quantify the gain of information over time of an attacker interacting with a differentially private query engine. In this book, we only consider sequential composition, in the more abstract form formalized below.

---

[1] The necessity of these were questioned in [17], where the authors showed a natural notions of anonymity that contradict them.

Definition 2.4 (*Composability*). A privacy definition Def with parameter α is composable if for any two mechanisms $\mathcal{M}_1$ and $\mathcal{M}_2$ satisfying respectively α_1-Def and α_2-Def, the mechanism $\mathcal{M}(D) = (\mathcal{M}_1(D), \mathcal{M}_2(D))$ satisfies α-Def for some (non-trivial) α which is a function of α_1 and α_2.

2.4 Relations Between Definitions

When learning about a new data privacy notion, it is often useful to know what are the known relations between this notion and other definitions. However, definitions have parameters that often have different meanings, and whose value is not directly comparable. To capture extensions, when a definition can be seen as a special case of another, we introduce the following definition.

Definition 2.5 (*Extensions*). Let α-Def$_1$ and β-Def$_2$ be data privacy definitions. We say that Def$_1$ is extended by Def$_2$, and denote is as Def$_1 \subset$ Def$_2$, if for all α, there is a value of β such that α-Def$_1$ is identical to β-Def$_2$.

Concerning variants, to claim that a definition is stronger than another, we adopt the concept of ordering established in [18] using α and β as tuples, encoding multiple parameters. Note that we slightly changed the original definition as that only required the second condition to hold, which would classify any extension as a stronger variant.

Definition 2.6 (*Relative strength of privacy definitions*). Let α-Def$_1$ and β-Def$_2$ be data privacy definitions. We say that Def$_1$ is stronger than Def$_2$, and denote it Def$_1 \succ$ Def$_2$, if:

- for all α, there is a β such that α-Def$_1 \implies \beta$-Def$_2$;
- for all β, there is an α such that α-Def$_1 \implies \beta$-Def$_2$.

If Def$_1$ is both stronger than and weaker than Def$_2$, we say that the two definitions are equivalent, and denote it Def$_1 \sim$ Def$_2$.

Relative strength implies a partial ordering on the space of possible definitions. On the other hand, if two definitions are equivalent, this does not mean that they are equal: They could be only equal up to a change in parameters. Both relations are reflexive and transitive; and we define the symmetric counterpart of these relations as well (i.e., $\prec$ and $\supset$). Moreover, for brevity, we combine these concepts in $\supset^{\succ}$, $\supset^{\prec}$, $\supset^{\sim}$, $\subset^{\succ}$, $\subset^{\prec}$, and $\subset^{\sim}$. For instance, if Def$_1 \subset$ Def$_2$ and Def$_1 \succ$ Def$_2$, we say that Def$_2$ is a weaker extension of Def$_1$ and denote it Def$_1 \subset^{\succ}$ Def$_2$.

Later in this book in Chap. 10, we summarize each definition and we also highlight its dimensions and its relation to other notions. Besides, we also specify whether these notions satisfy the privacy axioms and the composability property.

References

1. Stanley, L.W.: Randomized response: a survey technique for eliminating evasive answer bias. J. Am. Stat. Assoc. (1965)
2. Evfimievski, A., Gehrke, J., Srikant, R.: Limiting privacy breaches in privacy preserving data mining. In: Proceedings of the Twenty-Second ACM SIGMOD-SIGACT-SIGART Symposium on Principles of Database Systems. ACM (2003)
3. Dwork, C., McSherry, F.: Differential data privacy (2005)
4. Dwork, C.: Differential privacy. In: *Proceedings of the 33rd International Conference on Automata, Languages and Programming*. ACM (2006)
5. Dwork, C., McSherry, F., Nissim, K., Smith, A.: Calibrating noise to sensitivity in private data analysis. In: Theory of Cryptography Conference. Springer (2006)
6. Goldwasser, S., Micali, S.: Probabilistic encryption. J. Comput. Syst. Sci. (1984)
7. Chaudhuri, K., Mishra, N.: When random sampling preserves privacy. In: Annual International Cryptology Conference. Springer (2006)
8. Haitner, I., Mazor, N., Shaltiel, R., Silbak, J.: Channels of small log-ratio leakage and characterization of two-party differentially private computation. In: Theory of Cryptography Conference. Springer (2019)
9. Mireshghallah, F., Taram, M., Vepakomma, P., Singh, A., Raskar, R., Esmaeilzadeh, H.: Privacy in deep learning: a survey (2020). arXiv preprint arXiv:2004.12254
10. Papernot, N., Abadi, M., Erlingsson, U., Goodfellow, I., Talwar, K.: Semi-supervised knowledge transfer for deep learning from private training data (2016). arXiv preprint arXiv:1610.05755
11. Pejo, B., Tang, Q., Biczók, G.: Together or alone: The price of privacy in collaborative learning. In: Proceedings on Privacy Enhancing Technologies (2019)
12. Chaudhuri, K., Monteleoni, C., Sarwate, A.D.: Differentially private empirical risk minimization. J. Mach. Learn. Res. **12**(3) (2011)
13. Abadi, M., Chu, A., Goodfellow, I., Brendan McMahan, H., Mironov, I., Talwar, K., Zhang, L.: Deep learning with differential privacy. In: Proceedings of the 2016 ACM SIGSAC Conference on Computer and Communications Security, pp. 308–318 (2016)
14. Carl Tschantz, M., Sen, S., Datta, A.: Sok: differential privacy as a causal property. In: 2020 IEEE Symposium on Security and Privacy (SP) (2020)
15. Kifer, D., Lin, B.-R.: Towards an axiomatization of statistical privacy and utility. In: Proceedings of the twenty-ninth ACM SIGMOD-SIGACT-SIGART symposium on Principles of database systems. ACM (2010)
16. Kifer, D., Lin, B.-R.: An axiomatic view of statistical privacy and utility. J. Privacy Confidential. (2012)
17. Huber, M., Müller-Quade, J., Nilges, T: Defining privacy based on distributions of privacy breaches. In: Number Theory and Cryptography. Springer (2013)
18. Cuff, P., Yu, L.: Differential privacy as a mutual information constraint. In: Proceedings of the 2016 ACM SIGSAC Conference on Computer and Communications Security. ACM (2016)

Chapter 3
Quantification of Privacy Loss (Q)

The risk model associated to DP is a "worst-case" property: It quantifies not only over all possible neighboring datasets but also over all possible outputs. However, in many real-life risk assessments, events with vanishingly small probability are ignored or their risk weighted according to their probability. It is natural to consider analogous relaxations, especially since these relaxations often have better composition properties and enable mechanisms with better composition properties, like the Gaussian mechanism [1].

Most of the definitions within this chapter can be expressed using the *privacy loss random variable*, first defined in [2] as the *adversary's confidence gain*, so we first introduce this concept. Roughly speaking, it measures how much information is revealed by the output of a mechanism.

Definition 3.1 (*Privacy loss random variable* [2]). Let $\mathcal{M}$ be a mechanism, and D_1 and D_2 two datasets. The privacy loss random variable (PLRV) between $\mathcal{M}(D_1)$ and $\mathcal{M}(D_2)$ is defined as:

$$\mathcal{L}_{\mathcal{M}(D_1)/\mathcal{M}(D_2)}(O) = \ln\left(\frac{\mathbb{P}[\mathcal{M}(D_1) = O]}{\mathbb{P}[\mathcal{M}(D_2) = O]}\right)$$

If neither $\mathbb{P}[\mathcal{M}(D_1) = O]$ nor $\mathbb{P}[\mathcal{M}(D_2) = O]$ is 0; in case only $\mathbb{P}[\mathcal{M}(D_2) = O]$ is zero then $\mathcal{L}_{\mathcal{M}(D_1)/\mathcal{M}(D_2)}(O) = \infty$, otherwise $-\infty$. When the mechanism is clear from context, we simply write $\mathcal{L}_{D_1/D_2}$.

DP bounds the maximum value of $\mathcal{L}_{D_1/D_2}$. Instead of considering the maximum value, which corresponds to the worst possible output, relaxations of this chapter will allow a small probability of error, consider the average of the privacy loss random variable, or describe its behavior in finer ways.

© The Author(s), under exclusive license to Springer Nature Switzerland AG 2022
B. Pejó and D. Desfontaines, *Guide to Differential Privacy Modifications*,
SpringerBriefs in Computer Science,
https://doi.org/10.1007/978-3-030-96398-9_3

3.1   Allowing a Small Probability of Error

The first option, whose introduction is commonly attributed to [3], relaxes the definition of ε-indistinguishability by allowing an additional small density of probability on which the upper ε bound does not hold. This small density, denoted δ, can be used to compensate for outputs for which the privacy loss is larger than e^ε. This led to the definition of *approximate DP*, often simply called (ε, δ)-DP. This is, by far, the most commonly used relaxation in the scientific literature.

Definition 3.2 ((ε, δ)-*differential privacy* [3]). A privacy mechanism $\mathcal{M}$ is (ε, δ)-DP if for any datasets D_1 and D_2 that differ only on one record, and for all $S \subseteq \mathcal{O}$:

$$\mathbb{P}[\mathcal{M}(D_1) \in S] \leq e^\varepsilon \cdot \mathbb{P}[\mathcal{M}(D_2) \in S] + \delta$$

This definition is equivalent with *Max-KL stability* [4], a special case of algorithmic stability, which requires that one change in an algorithm's inputs does not change its output "too much."

The δ in (ε, δ)-DP is sometimes explained as the probability that the privacy loss of the output is larger than e^ε (or, equivalently, that the ε-indistinguishability formula is satisfied). In fact, this intuition corresponds to a different definition, first introduced in [5] as *probabilistic DP*, also called (ε, δ)-*DP in distribution* in [6]. Here, we present a simpler reformulation from [7].

Definition 3.3 ((ε, δ)-*probabilistic differential privacy* [7]). A privacy mechanism $\mathcal{M}$ is (ε, δ)-probabilistically DP (ProDP) if for any datasets D_1 and D_2 that differ only on one record there is a set $S_1 \subseteq \mathcal{O}$ where $\mathbb{P}[\mathcal{M}(D_1) \in S_1] \leq \delta$, such that for all measurable sets $S \subseteq \mathcal{O}$:

$$\mathbb{P}[\mathcal{M}(D_1) \in S \backslash S_1] \leq e^\varepsilon \cdot \mathbb{P}[\mathcal{M}(D_2) \in S \backslash S_1]$$

If we express these DP notions using the PLRV, the difference are quite intuitive:

$$\varepsilon\text{-DP} \quad\quad \Leftrightarrow \mathbb{P}_{O \sim \mathcal{M}(D_1)}\left[\mathcal{L}_{D_1/D_2}(O) > \varepsilon\right] = 0$$
$$(\varepsilon, \delta)\text{-DP} \quad \Leftrightarrow \mathbb{E}_{O \sim \mathcal{M}(D_1)}\left[\max\left(0, 1 - e^{\varepsilon - \mathcal{L}_{D_1/D_2}(O)}\right)\right] \leq \delta$$
$$(\varepsilon, \delta)\text{-ProDP} \Leftrightarrow \mathbb{P}_{O \sim \mathcal{M}(D_1)}\left[\mathcal{L}_{D_1/D_2}(O) > \varepsilon\right] \leq \delta$$

A more relaxed notion is *relaxed DP* [8] which require (ε, δ)-DP to hold only with some probability.

3.2   Averaging the Privacy Loss

As DP corresponds to a worst-case risk model, it is natural to consider relaxations to allow for larger privacy loss for some outputs. It is also natural to consider "average-case" risk models: allowing larger privacy loss values only if lower values compensate it in other cases.

One such relaxation is called *Kullback-Leibler privacy* [9, 10]: It considers the mean of the privacy loss random variable, which measures how much information is revealed when the output of a private algorithm is observed.

Definition 3.4 (*ε-Kullback–Leibler privacy* [9, 10]). A privacy mechanism $\mathcal{M}$ is *ε*-Kullback–Leibler private (KLPr) if for all D_1, D_2 differing in one record:

$$\mathbb{E}_{O \sim \mathcal{M}(D_1)} \left[\mathcal{L}_{D_1/D_2}(O) \right] \leq \varepsilon$$

ε-KL privacy considers the arithmetic mean of the privacy loss random variable or, equivalently, the geometric mean of $e^{\mathcal{L}_{D_1/D_2}}$. This choice of averaging function does not attribute a lot of weight to worst-case events, where $\mathcal{L}_{D_1/D_2}$ takes high values. *Rényi DP* extends this idea by adding a parameter $\alpha \geq 1$, which allows controlling the choice of averaging function by bounding the αth momentum of the privacy loss random variable.

Definition 3.5 (*(α, ε)-Rényi differential privacy* [11]). Given $\alpha > 1$, a privacy mechanism $\mathcal{M}$ is (α, ε)-Rényi DP if for all pairs of neighboring datasets D_1 and D_2:

$$\mathbb{E}_{O \sim \mathcal{M}(D_1)} \left[e^{(\alpha-1)\mathcal{L}_{D_1/D_2}(O)} \right] \leq e^{(\alpha-1)\varepsilon}$$

This definition can be naturally extended by continuity to $\alpha = 1$ (where it is equivalent to *ε*-KL privacy) and $\alpha = \infty$ (where it is equivalent to *ε*-DP). Larger values of α lead to more weight being assigned to worst-case events, i.e., (α, ε)-Rényi DP $\succ (\alpha', \varepsilon)$-Rényi DP iff $\alpha > \alpha'$.

Note that KL privacy and Rény DP can be expressed with the corresponding divergences: $D_{KL} (\mathcal{M}(D_1) | \mathcal{M}(D_2)) \leq \varepsilon$ where D_{KL} is the Kullback–Leibler divergence and $D_\alpha (\mathcal{M}(D_1) | \mathcal{M}(D_2)) \leq \varepsilon$ where D_α is the Rényi divergence of order α. Consequently, it is possible to use other divergence functions to obtain other relaxations. For example, in [12], the authors introduce two technical definitions, *binary-$|\chi|^\alpha$ DP* and *tenary-$|\chi|^\alpha$ DP*, as part of a proof on amplification by sampling. Other examples of divergences can lead to other variants, like *ε-total variation privacy* [9] and *quantum DP* [13], using the total variance and the quantum divergence respectively.

3.3 Controlling the Tail Distribution

Some definitions go further than simply considering a worst-case bound on the privacy loss, or averaging it across the distribution. They try to obtain the benefits of (ε, δ)-DP with a smaller ε which holds in most cases, but control the behavior of the bad cases better than (ε, δ)-DP, which allows for catastrophic privacy loss in rare cases.

The first attempt to formalize this idea was proposed in [14], where the authors introduce *mean-concentrated DP*. In this definition, a parameter controls the privacy loss variable globally and another parameter allows for some outputs to have a greater privacy loss, while still requiring that the difference is smaller than a Gaussian distribution. In [15], the authors criticize this definition and propose another formalization of the same idea called *zero-concentrated DP* [15], which requires that the privacy loss random variable is concentrated around zero.

Definition 3.6 ((ξ, ρ)*-zero-concentrated differential privacy* [15]). A mechanism $\mathcal{M}$ is (ξ, ρ)-zero-concentrated DP (zCoDP) if for all pairs of neighboring datasets D_1 and D_2 and all $\alpha > 1$:

$$\mathbb{E}_{O \sim \mathcal{M}(D_1)} \left[e^{(\alpha-1)\mathcal{L}_{D_1/D_2}(O)} \right] \leq e^{(\alpha-1)(\xi+\rho\alpha)}$$

Four more variants of concentrated DP exist. *Approximate zCoDP* [15], which relaxes zCoDP by only taking the Rényi divergence on events with high probability instead of on the full distribution. *Bounded CoDP* [15] relaxes zCoDP by requiring the inequality to hold only for the first few momentums. The final two definitions share the *truncated CoDP* name from [13, 16], where the first relaxes $(0, \rho)$-zCoDP in the same way as bonded CoDP and the second requires the Rényi divergence to be smaller than $\min(\xi, \alpha\tau)$ for all $\alpha \geq 1$.

3.4   Extension

Most definitions of this chapter can be seen as bounding the divergence between $\mathcal{M}(D_1)$ and $\mathcal{M}(D_2)$, for different possible divergence functions. In [9], the authors use this fact to generalize them and define (f, ε)-*divergence DP*, which takes the particular divergence used as a parameter f.

Definition 3.7 ((f, ε)*-divergence differential privacy* [9]). Let f be a convex function such as $f(1) = 0$. A privacy mechanism $\mathcal{M}$ is (f, ε)-divergence DP (DivDP) if for all pairs of neighboring datasets D_1, D_2:

$$\mathbb{E}_{O \sim \mathcal{M}(D_1)} \left[f \left(e^{\mathcal{L}_{D_1/D_2}} \right) \right] \leq \varepsilon$$

An instance of this definition was presented in [17] as (f_k, ε)-*divergence DP*, which requires that $\mathbb{E}_{O \sim \mathcal{M}(D_1)} \left[\left| e^{\mathcal{L}_{D_1/D_2}} - 1 \right|^k \right] \leq \varepsilon^k$. Moreover, *capacity bounded DP* was introduced in [18], which uses H-restricted f-divergence and requires the condition to hold only for a selected set of functions (queries) instead of all possible ones.

Finally, most definitions in this chapter can be extended to use a "family" of parameters (e.g., $(\varepsilon, \delta(\varepsilon))$) rather than a single pair. For instance in case of (ε, δ)-DP, ProDP, and Rényi DP, finding the tightest possible family of parameters for a given mechanism is equivalent to specifying the behavior of the corresponding PLRV [19].

3.5 Multidimensional Definitions

Allowing a small probability of error δ by using the same concept as in (ε, δ)-DP is very common; many new DP definitions were proposed in the literature with such a parameter. Unless it creates a particularly notable effect, we do not mention it explicitly and present the definitions without this parameter.

Definitions in this chapter can be used as standalone concepts: (ε, δ)-DP is omnipresent in the literature, and the principle of averaging risk is natural enough for RenyiDP to be used in practical settings. Most variants in this section, however, are only used as technical tools to get better results on composition or privacy amplification.

References

1. Dwork, C., Roth, A., et al.: The algorithmic foundations of differential privacy. In: Foundations and Trends® in Theoretical Computer Science (2014)
2. Dinur, I., Nissim, K.: Revealing information while preserving privacy. In: Proceedings of the Twenty-Second ACM SIGMOD-SIGACT-SIGART Symposium on Principles of Database Systems. ACM (2003)
3. Dwork, C., Kenthapadi, K., McSherry, F., Mironov, I., Naor, M.: Our Data, Ourselves: Privacy via Distributed Noise Generation. Springer, In Eurocrypt (2006)
4. Bassily, R., Nissim, K., Smith, A., Steinke, T., Stemmer, U., Ullman, J.: Algorithmic stability for adaptive data analysis. In: Proceedings of the Forty-Eighth Annual ACM Symposium on Theory of Computing. ACM (2016)
5. Machanavajjhala, A., Kifer, D., Abowd, J., Gehrke, J., Vilhuber, L.: Privacy: theory meets practice on the map. In: Proceedings of the 2008 IEEE 24th International Conference on Data Engineering. IEEE Computer Society (2008)
6. Canard, S., Olivier, B.: Differential privacy in distribution and instance-based noise mechanisms. In: IACR Cryptology ePrint Archive (2015)
7. Meiser, S.: Approximate and probabilistic differential privacy definitions. In: Cryptology ePrint Archive, Report 2018/277 (2018)
8. Zhang, Z., Qin, Z., Zhu, L., Jiang, W., Xu, C., Ren, K.: Toward practical differential privacy in smart grid with capacity-limited rechargeable batteries (2015)
9. Foygel Barber, R., Duchi, J.C.: Privacy and statistical risk: formalisms and minimax bounds. arXiv preprint arXiv:1412.4451 (2014)
10. Cuff, P., Yu, L.: Differential privacy as a mutual information constraint. In: Proceedings of the 2016 ACM SIGSAC Conference on Computer and Communications Security. ACM (2016)
11. Mironov, I.: Renyi differential privacy. In: 2017 IEEE 30th Computer Security Foundations Symposium (CSF). IEEE (2017)
12. Wang, Y.-X., Balle, B., Kasiviswanathan, S.P.: Subsampled rényi differential privacy and analytical moments accountant. In: The 22nd International Conference on Artificial Intelligence and Statistics, pp. 1226–1235. PMLR (2019)
13. Colisson, L.: L3 internship report: quantum analog of differential privacy in term of rényi divergence (2016)
14. Dwork, C., Rothblum, G.N.: Concentrated differential privacy. arXiv preprint arXiv:1603.01887 (2016)
15. Bun, M, Steinke, T.: Concentrated differential privacy: simplifications, extensions, and lower bounds. In: Theory of Cryptography Conference. Springer (2016)

16. Bun, M., Dwork, C., Rothblum, G.N., Steinke, T.: Composable and versatile privacy via truncated CDP. In: Proceedings of the 50th Annual ACM SIGACT Symposium on Theory of Computing. ACM (2018)
17. Duchi, J.C., Ruan, F.: The right complexity measure in locally private estimation: it is not the fisher information. arXiv preprintarXiv:1806.05756 (2018)
18. Chaudhuri, K., Imola, J., Machanavajjhala, A.: Capacity bounded differential privacy. In: Advances in Neural Information Processing Systems (2019)
19. Sommer, D.M., Meiser, S., Mohammadi, E.; Privacy loss classes: the central limit theorem in differential privacy. Proceedings on Privacy Enhancing Technologies (2019)

Chapter 4
Neighborhood Definition (N)

The original definition of DP considers datasets differing in one record. Thus, the datasets can differ in two possible ways: Either they have the same size and differ only on one record, or one is a copy of the other with one extra record. These two options do not protect the same thing: the former protects the "value" of the records, while the latter also protects their "presence" in the data: together, they protect any property about a single individual.

In many scenarios, it makes sense to protect a different property about their dataset, e.g., the value of a specific sensitive field, or entire groups of individuals. It is straightforward to adapt DP to protect different sensitive properties: All one has to do is change the definition of neighborhood in the original definition.

4.1 Changing the Sensitive Property

The original definition states that the ε-indistinguishability property should hold for "any datasets D_1 and D_2 that differ only on the data of one individual." Modifying the set of pairs (D_1, D_2) such that $\mathcal{M}(D_1) \approx_\varepsilon \mathcal{M}(D_2)$ is equivalent to changing the protected sensitive property.

Weaker relaxations
In DP, the difference between D_1 and D_2 is sometimes interpreted as "one record value is different," or "one record has been added or removed." In [1], the authors formalize these two options as *bounded DP* and *unbounded DP*. They also introduced *attribute DP* and *bit DP*, for smaller changes within the differing record.

Definition 4.1 ([1]). If a privacy mechanism $\mathcal{M}$ satisfies $\mathcal{M}(D_1) \approx_\varepsilon \mathcal{M}(D_2)$ for any pair D_1, D_2, where D_1 can be obtained from D_2 by …
- …adding or removing one record, then $\mathcal{M}$ is ε-unbounded DP (uBoDP).
- …changing exactly one record, then $\mathcal{M}$ is ε-bounded DP (BoDP).

© The Author(s), under exclusive license to Springer Nature Switzerland AG 2022   19
B. Pejó and D. Desfontaines, *Guide to Differential Privacy Modifications*,
SpringerBriefs in Computer Science,
https://doi.org/10.1007/978-3-030-96398-9_4

- ...changing one attribute in a record, then $\mathcal{M}$ is ε-attribute DP (AttDP).
- ...changing one bit of an attribute in a record, then $\mathcal{M}$ is ε-bit DP (BitDP).

The original definition of ε-DP is the conjunction of ε-uBoDP and ε-bDP. However, bounded DP is frequently used in the literature, especially when using local DP, and often simply called DP. It is also sometimes renamed, like in [2], where the authors call it *per-person DP*.

Another way to relax the neighborhood definition in DP is to consider that only certain types of information are sensitive. For example, if the attacker learns that their target has cancer, this is more problematic than if they learn that their target does not have cancer. This idea is captured in *one-sided DP* [3]: The neighbors of a dataset D are obtained by replacing a single sensitive record with any other record (sensitive or not). The idea of sensitivity is captured by a policy P, which specifies which records are sensitive. This idea cannot be captured by ε-indistinguishability, since one-sided DP is asymmetric.

Definition 4.2 ((P, ε)-one-sided differential privacy [3]). Given a policy $P \subseteq \mathcal{T}$, a privacy mechanism $\mathcal{M}$ is (P, ε)-one-sided DP (OSDP) if for all datasets D_1 and D_2, where D_2 has been obtained by replacing a record $t \in D_1 \cap P$ by any other record and for all $S \subseteq \mathcal{O}$:

$$\mathbb{P}[\mathcal{M}(D_1) \in S] \leq e^{\varepsilon} \cdot \mathbb{P}[\mathcal{M}(D_2) \in S]$$

Similar ideas are proposed in multiple papers. In [4], the authors propose *asymetric DP*, which is the unbounded version of OSDP. In [5], the authors propose *sensitive privacy*, which determines which records are sensitive based on the data itself and a normality property instead of using a data-independent determination. In [6], the authors introduce *anomaly-restricted DP*, which assumes that there is only one outlier in the dataset and that this outlier should not be protected.

Stronger notions
More restrictive definitions are also possible. First, some definitions make the definition of neighborhood more explicit when a single person can contribute multiple times to a dataset; this is the case for *client/user/participant DP*, defined in [7]. Some works also argue that in-between definitions are appropriate: rather than protecting a single contribution or entire users contributions. The authors in [8] suggest that protecting elements that reveal information about users, after deduplicating or clustering contributions. They call the corresponding definition *element-level DP*.

In [9], the authors implicitly define (c, ε)-*group privacy* considers datasets that do not differ in one record, but possibly several, to protect multiple individuals. This can also be interpreted as taking correlations into account when using DP: *DP under correlation* [10] uses an extra parameter to describe the maximum number of records that the change of one individual can influence.

These two definitions are formally equivalent, but the implicit interpretation of DP behind them is different. (c, ε)-group privacy is compatible with the associative view under the strong adversary assumption (the adversary knows all records except *c*) or the causal view (*c* records are changed after the data is generated). Meanwhile, DP under correlation implicitly considers the associative view with the independence assumption and tries to relax that assumption. This last approach was further developed via *dependent DP* [11], which uses dependence relationships to describe how much the variation in one record can influence the other records.

Definition 4.3 ((R, c, ε)-dependent differential privacy [11]). A privacy mechanism $\mathcal{M}$ provides (R, c, ε)-dependent DP where R is the probabilistic dependence relationship and c is the dependence size, if for any pair of datasets D_1 and D_2, where D_2 has been obtained from D_1 by changing one record and the corresponding at most $c - 1$ other records according to R, $\mathcal{M}(D_1) \approx_\varepsilon \mathcal{M}(D_2)$.

Similar definitions appear in [12, 13] as *correlated indistinguishability* and *correlated tuple DP*, respectively, in which correlations are defined by a correlation matrix. The authors in [14, 15] also considered correlation and defined as *correlated DP*, where the correlations are defined by an observation on other datasets. Furthermore, in [16] as *bayesian DP*[1], where the neighborhood relation is defined by an adversary having some knowledge about correlations in the data. An extension of the latter is proposed in [19] as *prior DP* which considers a family of adversaries instead of a single adversary.

The strongest possible variant is considered in [1], where the authors define *free lunch privacy*, in which the attacker must be unable to distinguish between any two datasets, even if they are completely different. This guarantee is a reformulation of Dalenius' privacy goal [20]; as such, all mechanisms that satisfy free lunch privacy have a near-total lack of utility.

Definition 4.4 (ε-free lunch privacy [1]). A privacy mechanism $\mathcal{M}$ satisfies ε-free lunch privacy (FLPr) if $\mathcal{M}(D_1) \approx_\varepsilon \mathcal{M}(D_2)$ for any pair of datasets D_1, D_2.

4.2 Limiting the Scope of the Definition

Redefining the neighborhood property can also be used to reduce the scope of the definitions. In [21], the authors note that DP requires ε-indistinguishability of results between any pair of neighboring datasets, but in practice, the data custodian has only one dataset D they want to protect. Thus, they only require ε-indistinguishability between this dataset D and all its neighbors, calling the resulting definition *individual DP*. An equivalent definition was proposed in [22] as *conditioned DP*.

Definition 4.5 ((D, ε)-individual differential privacy [21]). Given a dataset $D \in \mathcal{D}$, a privacy mechanism $\mathcal{M}$ satisfies (D, ε)-individual DP (InDP) if for any dataset D' that differs in at most one record from D, $\mathcal{M}(D) \approx_\varepsilon \mathcal{M}(D')$.

---

[1] There are two other notions with the same name: introduced in [17, 18], we mention them in Chap. 5 and 6, respectively.

This definition was further restricted in *per-instance DP* [23] where besides fixing a dataset D, the different record t is also fixed.

4.3   Considering Other Types of Input

Many adaptations of DP are simply changing the neighborhood definition to protect different types of input data than datasets. A few examples follow.

Location
In [24], the authors defined *location privacy*, in which neighbors are datasets which differ in at most one record, and the two differing records are at a physical distance smaller than a given threshold. This definition also appears in [25] as *DP on r-location set*.[2] Several more location-related DP variants were defined in [27]: *untrackability* (which adopts differential privacy for set of locations by protecting whether they originated from a single user or by two users), *undetectability* and *multi user untrackability*, (which extend this idea further by not assuming both sets originated from the same private data and to multiple users, respectively).

Graph
In [28], the authors adopt DP to graph-structured data and present multiple alternative definitions, which protect different parts of the graph: The strongest is *node-DP*, which protects a node and all its edges; the weakest is *edge-DP*, only protects one edge; and an intermediate definition is *k-edge-DP*, which protects a total of k edges and nodes. Similarly to one-sided DP, in [29, 30], the authors introduce *out-link privacy*, and *protected DP* which protects all outgoing edges from a given node and guarantees that no observer can learn much about the set of edges corresponding to any protected node, respectively. In addition, in [31], the author introduces *QL-edged-labeled DP* which only protecting a predetermined subset of outgoing edges. In [32], the author introduces *l_1-weighted DP*, in which graph edges are weighted, and graphs are neighbors when the total weight of their differing edges is smaller than 1; this notion was also defined implicitly in [33]. In [34], the authors defined *feasible node-DP* for control-flow graphs where an addition or removal of a node results in a feasible run-time behaviors. In [35], the authors define *decentralized DP* which extends the graph neighborhood to two jumps. Finally, in [36] the authors introduce *seamless privacy*, which rather than protecting characteristics of a specific input graph, it ensures that certain pairs of queries on this graph return similar answers.

Stream
Several authors adapt DP to a streaming context, where the attacker can access the mechanism's internal states. In [37–39], authors define *pan-privacy*, which comes in two variants: *event-level* pan-privacy (called *strong DP* in [40]) protects individual events, and *user-level* pan-privacy protects all events associated to a single user. In

---

[2] Distinct from *DP on δ-location set* [26], which we mention in Chap. 5.

[41], the authors extend the previous idea and propose *w-event privacy*, which protects any event sequence occurring within a window of at most w timestamps. In [27, 42], this was further extended to an infinite horizon via *discounted DP* (which keep assigning smaller-and-smaller weights to further-and-further events) and *everlasting privacy* (which limit the leakage of information users suffer, no matter how many executions a mechanism had), respectively. Finally, *series-indistinguishability* [43] captured data correlations in the streaming context and the authors in [44, 45] adopted DP for Kalman filters and to time-independent power spectral densities respectively.

RAM and PIR
In [46], the authors adopt DP for random access memory and private information retrieval. For RAM, the neighborhood is defined over the sequence of logical memory requests over time; the same notion appears in [47] as *differential obliviousness* and in [48] as *oblivious DP*. The adaptation of neighborhood is similar in case of PIR; a similar notion appears in [49] as *ε-private PIR* and in [50] as *ε-DPIR*. Additionally, in [51], the authors use a similar idea to define DP for outsourced database systems.

Text and Images
In [52], the authors adapt DP for symbolic control systems and introduce *word-DP* and *substitution-word-DP*, protecting respectively pairs of words whose Levenshtein distance is lower than a given parameter, or whose Hamming distance is lower than a given parameter. In [53], the authors adapt DP for text vectors, and propose *text indistinguishability*, in which the neighborhood relationship between two word vectors depends on their Euclidean distance. In [54–56], the authors define *refinement DP*, *DP Image*, and *Pixel DP*, respectively, which adopts the definition for images with neighbors given by some transformation or metric.

Miscellaneous
Beside the already mentioned fields, DP was adopted to numerous other use cases, such as for set operations in [57], for gossip protocols in [58], for functions in [59], for genomic data in [60], for recommendation systems in [61], for machine learning in [62], and for bandit algorithms in [63, 64].

4.4 Extensions

It is natural to generalize the variants of this chapter to arbitrary neighboring relationships. One example is mentioned in [1], under the name *generic DP*,[3] where the neighboring relation is entirely captured by a relation $\mathcal{R}$ between datasets.

Definition 4.6 (($\mathcal{R}, \varepsilon$)-generic differential privacy [1]). Given a relation $\mathcal{R} \subseteq \mathcal{D}^2$, a privacy mechanism $\mathcal{M}$ satisfies ($\mathcal{R}, \varepsilon$)-generic DP (GcDP) if for all $(D_1, D_2) \in \mathcal{R}$, $\mathcal{M}(D_1) \approx_\varepsilon \mathcal{M}(D_2)$.

This definition is symmetric, but it can easily be modified to accommodate asymmetric definitions like one-sided DP. Other definitions use different formalizations

---

[3] Another definition with the same name is introduced in [65, 66], we mention it in Chap. 5.

to also generalize the concept of changing the neighborhood relationship. Some (like pufferfish privacy, mentioned in Chap. 6) use "pairs of predicates" (ϕ_1, ϕ_2) that D_1 and D_2 must respectively satisfy to be neighbors. Others (like coupled-worlds privacy, mentioned in Chap. 8) use "private functions," denoted priv, and define neighbors to be datasets D_1 and D_2 such as $\mathsf{priv}(D_1) \neq \mathsf{priv}(D_2)$.

Others use a "distance function" d between datasets, and neighbors are defined as datasets a distance lower than a given threshold Δ; this is the case for *DP under a neighborhood*, introduced in [67], *adjacent DP*, introduced in [68],[4] and *constrained DP* introduced in [69]. Another definition coined by [69] is *distributional privacy*,[5] where there are additional constraints on the neighborhood definition: neighboring datasets must be part of a fixed set $S_{\mathcal{D}}$ and have elements in common. This distance can also be defined as the sensitivity of the mechanism, like in *sensitivity-induced DP* [72], or implicitly defined by a set of constraints, like what is done in [1] via *induced neighbors DP*.

One notable instantiation of generic DP is *blowfish privacy* [73]. Its major building blocks are a policy graph G that specifies which pairs of domain values in $\mathcal{T}$ should not be distinguished between by an adversary; and a set of constraints Q that specifies the set $\mathcal{I}_Q$ of possible datasets that the definition protects. It was inspired by the Pufferfish framework [74] (see Chap. 6), but the attacker is not assumed to have uncertainty over the data: Instead, it models an attacker whose knowledge is a set of deterministic constraints on the data.

Definition 4.7 (($(G, \mathcal{I}_Q, \varepsilon)$-blowfish privacy [73]). Given a policy graph $G \in \mathcal{T}^2$ and a set of datasets $\mathcal{I}_Q$, a privacy mechanism $\mathcal{M}$ satisfies (G, ε)-blowfish privacy if for all datasets D_1 and D_2 in $\mathcal{I}_Q$ that differ in only one element i such that $(D_1(i), D_2(i)) \in G$, $\mathcal{M}(D_1) \approx_{\varepsilon} \mathcal{M}(D_2)$.

4.5 Multidimensional Definitions

Modifying the protected property is orthogonal to modifying the risk model implied by the quantification of privacy loss: It is straightforward to combine these two dimensions. Indeed, many definitions mentioned in this chapter were actually introduced with a δ parameter allowing for a small probability of error. One-one particularly general and specific example is *adjacency relation divergence DP* [75], and *node-Rényi DP* [76], which combines an arbitrary neighborhood definition (like in generic DP) with an arbitrary divergence function (like in divergence DP) and adopts Rényi DP to graphs, respectively.

It is very common to change the definition of neighborhood in practical contexts to adapt what aspect of the data is protected. Further, local DP (see Chap. 11) mechanisms implicitly use bounded DP: The participation of one individual is not secret;

---

[4] Originally simply called DP by its authors.

[5] Another definition with the same name is introduced in [70, 71], we mention it in Chap. 5.

only the value of their record is protected. Variants that limit the scope of the definition to one particular dataset or user, however, provide few formal guarantees and do not seem to be used in practice.

References

1. Kifer, D., Machanavajjhala, A.: No free lunch in data privacy. In: Proceedings of the 2011 ACM SIGMOD International Conference on Management of data. ACM (2011)
2. Feldman, V., Mironov, I., Talwar, K., Thakurta, A.: Privacy amplification by iteration. In: 2018 IEEE 59th Annual Symposium on Foundations of Computer Science (FOCS). IEEE (2018)
3. Kotsogiannis, I., Doudalis, S., Haney, S., Machanavajjhala, A., Mehrotra, S.: One-sided differential privacy. In: 2020 IEEE 36th International Conference on Data Engineering (ICDE), pp. 493–504. IEEE (2020)
4. Takagi, S., Cao, Y., Yoshikawa, M.: Asymmetric differential privacy. arXiv preprint arXiv:2103.00996 (2021)
5. Asif, H., Papakonstantinou, P.A., Vaidya, J.: How to accurately and privately identify anomalies. In: Proceedings of the 2019 ACM SIGSAC Conference on Computer and Communications Security. ACM (2019)
6. Bittner, D. M., Sarwate, A.D., Wright, R.N.: Using noisy binary search for differentially private anomaly detection. In: International Symposium on Cyber Security Cryptography and Machine Learning. Springer (2018)
7. McMahan, H.B., Ramage, D., Talwar, K., Zhang, L.: Learning differentially private recurrent language models. In: International Conference on Learning Representations (2018)
8. Asi, H., Duchi, J., Javidbakht, O.: Element level differential privacy: The right granularity of privacy. arXiv preprint arXiv:1912.04042 (2019)
9. Dwork, C.: Differential privacy: a survey of results. In: International Conference on Theory and Applications of Models of Computation. Springer (2008)
10. Chen, R., Fung, B.C., Yu, P.S., Desai, B.C.: Correlated network data publication via differential privacy. VLDB J. Int. J. Very Large Data Bases (2014)
11. Liu, C: Chakraborty, Supriyo: and Prateek Mittal. Differential privacy under dependent tuples. In: NDSS, Dependence makes you vulnerable (2016)
12. Wang, H., Wang, H.: Correlated tuple data release via differential privacy. Inf. Sci. **560**, 347–369 (2021)
13. Wang, H., Wang, H.: Differentially private publication for correlated non-numerical data. Comput. J. (2021)
14. Wu, X., Dou, W., Ni, Q.: Game theory based privacy preserving analysis in correlated data publication. In: Proceedings of the Australasian Computer Science Week Multiconference. ACM (2017)
15. Wu, X., Wu, T., Khan, M., Ni, Q., Dou, W.: Game theory based correlated privacy preserving analysis in big data. IEEE Trans. Big Data (2017)
16. Yang, B., Sato, I., Nakagawa, H.: Bayesian differential privacy on correlated data. In: Proceedings of the 2015 ACM SIGMOD International Conference on Management of Data. ACM (2015)
17. Triastcyn, A., Faltings, B.: Bayesian differential privacy for machine learning. In: International Conference on Machine Learning, pp. 9583–9592. PMLR (2020)
18. Leung, S., Lui, E.: Bayesian Mechanism Design with Efficiency, Privacy, and Approximate Truthfulness. In: International Workshop on Internet and Network Economics. Springer (2012)
19. Li, Y., Ren, X., Yang, S., Yang, X.: Impact of prior knowledge and data correlation on privacy leakage: A unified analysis. IEEE Trans. Inf. Forensics Secur. (2019)
20. Dalenius, T.: Towards a methodology for statistical disclosure control. statistik Tidskrift (1977)

21. Soria-Comas, J., Domingo-Ferrer, J., Sánchez, D., Megías, D.: Individual differential privacy: a utility-preserving formulation of differential privacy guarantees. IEEE Trans. Inf. Forensics Secur. (2017)
22. Charest, A.-S., Hou, Y.: On the meaning and limits of empirical differential privacy. J. Priv. Confidential. (2016)
23. Redberg, R., Wang, Y.-X.: Privately publishable per-instance privacy. In:NeurIPS 2020 Competition and Demonstration Track. PMLR (2021)
24. ElSalamouny, E., Gambs, S.: Differential privacy models for location-based services. Trans. Data Priv. (2016)
25. Chen, Z., Bao, X., Ying, Z., Liu, X., Zhong, H.: Differentially private location protection with continuous time stamps for vanets. In: International Conference on Algorithms and Architectures for Parallel Processing. Springer (2018)
26. Xiao, Y., Xiong, L.: Protecting locations with differential privacy under temporal correlations. In: Proceedings of the 22nd ACM SIGSAC Conference on Computer and Communications Security. ACM (2015)
27. Naor, M., Vexler, N.: Can two walk together: privacy enhancing methods and preventing tracking of users. In: 1st Symposium on Foundations of Responsible Computing (FORC 2020). Schloss Dagstuhl-Leibniz-Zentrum für Informatik (2020)
28. Hay, M., Li, C., Miklau, G., Jensen, D.: Accurate estimation of the degree distribution of private networks. In: Ninth IEEE International Conference on Data Mining, 2009. ICDM'09. IEEE (2009)
29. Task, C., Clifton, C.: A guide to differential privacy theory in social network analysis. In: Proceedings of the 2012 International Conference on Advances in Social Networks Analysis and Mining (ASONAM 2012). IEEE Computer Society (2012)
30. Kearns, M., Roth, A., Wu, Z.S., Yaroslavtsev, G.: Private algorithms for the protected in social network search. Proc Natl Acad Sci (2016)
31. Reuben, J.: Towards a differential privacy theory for edge-labeled directed graphs. In: SICHER-HEIT (2018)
32. Pinot, R.: Minimum spanning tree release under differential privacy constraints. arXiv preprint arXiv:1801.06423 (2018)
33. Sealfon, A.: Shortest paths and distances with differential privacy. In: Proceedings of the 35th ACM SIGMOD-SIGACT-SIGAI Symposium on Principles of Database Systems. ACM (2016)
34. Zhang, H., Latif, S., Bassily, R., Rountev, A.: Differentially-private control-flow node coverage for software usage analysis. In: USENIX Security Symposium, pp. 1021–1038 (2020)
35. Sun, H., Xiao, X., Khalil, I., Yang, Y., Qin, Z., Wang, H.W., Yu, T.: Analyzing subgraph statistics from extended local views with decentralized differential privacy. In: Proceedings of the 2019 ACM SIGSAC Conference on Computer and Communications Security. ACM (2019)
36. Ding, X., Wang, W., Wan, M., Gu, M.: Seamless privacy: privacy-preserving subgraph counting in interactive social network analysis. In: 2013 International Conference on Cyber-Enabled Distributed Computing and Knowledge Discovery (CyberC). IEEE (2013)
37. Dwork, C., Naor, M., Pitassi, T., Rothblum, G.N.: Differential privacy under continual observation. In: Proceedings of the Forty-Second ACM Symposium on Theory of Computing. ACM (2010)
38. Dwork, C., Naor, M., Pitassi, T., Rothblum, G.N., Yekhanin, S.: Pan-private streaming algorithms. In: ICS (2010)
39. Dwork, C.: Differential privacy in new settings. In: Proceedings of the Twenty-First Annual ACM-SIAM Symposium on Discrete Algorithms. SIAM (2010)
40. Wang, Y., Sibai, H., Mitra, S., Dullerud, G.E.: Differential privacy for sequential algorithms (2020). arXiv preprint arXiv:2004.00275
41. Kellaris, G., Papadopoulos, S., Xiao, X., Papadias, D.: Differentially private event sequences over infinite streams. In: Proceedings of the VLDB Endowment (2014)
42. Farokhi, F.: Discounted differential privacy: privacy of evolving datasets over an infinite horizon. In: ACM/IEEE International Conference on Cyber-Physical Systems (ICCPS), Sydney, Australia (2020)

43. Wang, H., Zhengquan, X..: Cts-dp: publishing correlated time-series data via differential privacy. Knowl.-Based Syst. **122**, 167–179 (2017)
44. Le Ny, J., Pappas, G.J.: Differentially private filtering. IEEE Trans. Automat. Control **59**(2), 341–354 (2013)
45. Parker, K., Hale, M., Barooah, P.: Application to smart meter data. IEEE Internet Things J. Spectral differential privacy (2021)
46. Wagh, S., Cuff, P., Mittal, P.: Differentially private oblivious ram. In: Proceedings on Privacy Enhancing Technologies (2018)
47. Hubert Chan, T.H., Chung, K.-M., Maggs, B.M., Shi, E.: Foundations of differentially oblivious algorithms. In: Proceedings of the Thirtieth Annual ACM-SIAM Symposium on Discrete Algorithms. SIAM (2019)
48. Allen, J., Ding, B., Kulkarni, J., Nori, H., Ohrimenko, O., Yekhanin, S.: An algorithmic framework for differentially private data analysis on trusted processors. In: Advances in Neural Information Processing Systems (2019)
49. Toledo, R.R., Danezis, G., Goldberg, I.: Lower-cost ε-private information retrieval. In: Proceedings on Privacy Enhancing Technologies (2016)
50. Patel, S., Persiano, G., Yeo, K.: What storage access privacy is achievable with small overhead? In: Proceedings of the 38th ACM SIGMOD-SIGACT-SIGAI Symposium on Principles of Database Systems (2019)
51. Kellaris, G., Kollios, G., Nissim, K., O'Neill, A.: Accessing data while preserving privacy (2017). arXiv preprint arXiv:1706.01552
52. Jones, A., Leahy, K., Hale, M.: Towards differential privacy for symbolic systems. In: 2019 American Control Conference (ACC). IEEE (2019)
53. Zhang, J., Sun, J., Zhang, R., Zhang, Y., Hu, X.: Privacy-preserving social media data outsourcing. In: IEEE INFOCOM 2018-IEEE Conference on Computer Communications. IEEE (2018)
54. Ying, X., Wu, X., Wang, Y.: On linear refinement of differential privacy-preserving query answering. In: Pacific-Asia Conference on Knowledge Discovery and Data Mining. Springer (2013)
55. Fan, L.: Image pixelization with differential privacy. In: IFIP Annual Conference on Data and Applications Security and Privacy, pp. 148–162. Springer (2018)
56. Liu, B., Ding, M., Xue, H., Zhu, T., Ye, D., Song, L., Zhou, W.: Dp-image: differential privacy for image data in feature space. arXiv preprint arXiv:2103.07073 (2021)
57. Yan, Z., Liu, J., Li, G., Han, Z., Qiu, S.: Privmin: differentially private minhash for jaccard similarity computation. arXiv preprint arXiv:1705.07258 (2017)
58. Huang, Y., Dai, H.: Quantifying differential privacy of gossip protocols in general networks (2019). arXiv preprint arXiv:1905.07598
59. Nozari, E.: Networked dynamical systems: privacy, control, and cognition. Ph.D. thesis, UC San Diego (2019)
60. Simmons, S., Sahinalp, C., Berger, B.: Enabling privacy-preserving GWASS in heterogeneous human populations. Cell Syst (2016)
61. Guerraoui, R., Kermarrec, A.-M., Patra, R., Taziki, M.: D 2 p: distance-based differential privacy in recommenders. Proceedings of the VLDB Endowment (2015)
62. Long, Y., Bindschaedler, V., Gunter, C.A.: Towards measuring membership privacy. Unknown J. (2017)
63. Tossou, A.C.Y., Dimitrakakis, C.: Algorithms for differentially private multi-armed bandits. In: Thirtieth AAAI Conference on Artificial Intelligence (2016)
64. Basu, D., Dimitrakakis, C., Tossou, A.: Differential privacy for multi-armed bandits: What is it and what is its cost? (2019) arXiv preprint arXiv:1905.12298
65. Kifer, D., Lin, B.-R.: Towards an axiomatization of statistical privacy and utility. In: Proceedings of the Twenty-Ninth ACM SIGMOD-SIGACT-SIGART Symposium on Principles of Database Systems. ACM (2010)
66. Kifer, D., Lin, B.-R.: An axiomatic view of statistical privacy and utility. J. Privacy Confidential. (2012)

67. Fang, C., Chang, E.-C.: Differential privacy with delta-neighbourhood for spatial and dynamic datasets. In: Proceedings of the 9th ACM Symposium on Information, Computer and Communications Security. ACM (2014)
68. Krishnan, V.: Martínez, Sonia: a probabilistic framework for moving-horizon estimation: Stability and privacy guarantees. IEEE Trans. Autom. Control **66**(4), 1817–1824 (2020)
69. Zhou, S., Ligett, K., Wasserman, L.: Differential privacy with compression. In: IEEE International Symposium on Information Theory: ISIT 2009. IEEE (2009)
70. Roth, A.: New algorithms for preserving differential privacy. Microsoft Res. (2010)
71. Blum, A., Ligett, K., Roth, A.: A learning theory approach to noninteractive database privacy. J. ACM (JACM) (2013)
72. Rubinstein, B.I.P., Aldà, F.: Pain-free random differential privacy with sensitivity sampling. In: Proceedings of the 34th International Conference on Machine Learning, vol. 70. JMLR. org (2017)
73. He, X., Machanavajjhala, A., Ding, B.: Blowfish privacy: tuning privacy-utility trade-offs using policies. In: Proceedings of the 2014 ACM SIGMOD International Conference on Management of Data. ACM (2014)
74. Kifer, D., Machanavajjhala, A.: A rigorous and customizable framework for privacy. In: Proceedings of the 31st ACM SIGMOD-SIGACT-SIGAI Symposium on Principles of Database Systems. ACM (2012)
75. Kawamoto, Y., Murakami, T.: Local distribution obfuscation via probability coupling. In: 2019 57th Annual Allerton Conference on Communication, Control, and Computing (Allerton). IEEE (2019)
76. Daigavane, A., Madan, G., Sinha, A., Guha, A.H., Aggarwal, G.., Jain, P.: Node-level differential private graph neural networks. arXiv preprint arXiv:2111.15521 (2021)

Chapter 5
Variation of Privacy Loss (V)

In DP, the privacy parameter ε is "uniform": The level of protection is the same for all protected users or attributes, or equivalently, only the level of risk for the most at-risk user is considered. In practice, some users might require a higher level of protection than others or a data custodian might want to consider the level of risk across all users, rather than only considering the worst case. Some definitions take this into account by allowing the privacy loss to vary across inputs, either explicitly (by associating each user to an acceptable level of risk), or implicitly (by allowing some users to be at risk, or averaging the risk across users).

5.1 Allocating Different Privacy Levels

In Chap. 4, we saw how changing the definition of the neighborhood can be used to adapt the definition of privacy and protect different aspects of the input data. However, the privacy protection in those variants is binary: Either a given property is protected, or it was not. A possible option to generalize this idea further is to allow the privacy level to vary across possible inputs.

One natural example is to consider that some users might have higher privacy requirements than others and make the ε vary according to which user differs between the two datasets. This is done in *personalized DP*, a notion first defined informally in [1], then independently in [2–5]. An equivalent notion is also defined in [6] as *heterogeneous DP*.

Definition 1 [Ψ-personalized differential privacy [2–5]] A mechanism $\mathcal{M}$ satisfies Ψ-personalized DP (PerDP) for $\Psi : \mathcal{T} \to \mathbb{R}_0^\infty$ if for any dataset D, $\mathcal{M}(D) \approx_{\Psi(D(i))} \mathcal{M}(D_{-i})$.

This definition can be seen as a refinement of the intuition behind one-sided DP, which separated records into sensitive and non-sensitive ones. The idea of making the privacy level vary across inputs can be generalized further, by also making the privacy level depend on the entire dataset, and not only in the differing record. This is done in [7], where the authors define *tailored DP*.

Definition 2 (Ψ-*tailored differential privacy* [7]) A mechanism $\mathcal{M}$ satisfies Ψ-tailored DP (TaiDP) for $\Psi : \mathcal{T} \times \mathcal{D} \to \mathbb{R}_0^\infty$ if for any dataset D, $\mathcal{M}(D) \approx_{\Psi(D(i),D)} \mathcal{M}(D_{-i})$.

A similar notion is *input-discriminative DP* [8] where Ψ takes the two ε values corresponding to the two dataset. The authors also defined *minID-DP* where Ψ is the minimum function.

The concept of personalization can be applied to strengthen or weaken the privacy requirement for a record depending on whether they are an outlier in the dataset. In [7], the authors formalize this idea and introduce *outlier privacy*, which tailors an individual's protection level to their "outlierness." Other refinements are also introduced, such as *simple outlier privacy*, *simple outlier DP*, and *staircase outlier privacy*. A similar idea was explored in [9], which introduced *Pareto DP*: It utilizes a Pareto distribution of parameters (p, r) to separate a large number of low-frequency individuals from a small number of high-frequency individuals, and the sensitivity is calculated based on only the low-frequency individuals.

5.2   Randomizing the Privacy Levels

Varying the privacy level across inputs can also be done in a randomized way, by guaranteeing that some random fraction of users have a certain privacy level. One example is proposed in [10] as *random DP*: The authors note that rather than requiring DP to hold for any possible datasets, it is natural to only consider "realistic datasets," and allow "edge-case" or very unrealistic datasets to not be protected. This is captured by generating the data randomly and allowing a small proportion γ of cases to not satisfy the ε-indistinguishability property.

Definition 3 $((\pi, \gamma, \varepsilon)$-*random differential privacy* [10]] Let π be a probability distribution on $\mathcal{T}$, D_1 a dataset generated by drawing n i.i.d. elements in π, and D_2 the same dataset as D_1, except one element was changed to a new element drawn from π. A mechanism $\mathcal{M}$ is $(\pi, \gamma, \varepsilon)$-random DP RanDP) if $\mathcal{M}(D_1) \approx_\varepsilon \mathcal{M}(D_2)$, with probability at least $1 - \gamma$ on the choice of D_1 and D_2.

The exact meaning of "with probability at least $1 - \gamma$ on the choice of D_1 and D_2" can vary slightly. In [11, 12], the authors introduce *predictive DP* and *model-specific DP*, respectively, which quantify over all possible choices of D_1, and picks D_2 randomly in the neighborhood of D_1. In [13], D_1 and D_2 are both taken out of a set of density larger than $1 - \gamma$, and the authors call this definition *generalized DP*. The distribution generating the dataset is also not always assumed to be generating i.i.d. records; we denote the corresponding parameter by θ.

Random DP might look similar to probabilistic DP as in both cases there is a small probability that the privacy loss is unbounded. On the other hand, they are very different: In RanDP, this probability is computed inputs of the mechanisms (i.e., users or datasets), and for ProDP, it is computed across mechanism outputs. Also, similarly to ProDP, excluding some cases altogether creates definitional issues as RanDP also does not satisfy the convexity axiom.

Usually, data-generating distributions are used for other purposes: They typically model an adversary with partial knowledge. However, definitions in this chapter still compare the outputs of the mechanisms given fixed neighboring datasets: The only randomness in the indistinguishability property comes from the mechanism. By contrast, definitions of Chap. 6 compare the output of the mechanism on a random dataset, so the randomness comes both from the data-generating distribution and the mechanism.

5.3 Multidimensional Definitions

As varying the privacy level or limiting the considered datasets are two distinct way of relaxing DP, it is possible to combine them with the previously mentioned dimensions.

Combination with N

The definitions described in Chap. 4 have the same privacy constraint for all neighboring datasets. Thus, they cannot capture definitions that vary the privacy level across inputs. On the other hand, they can be combined quite easily. For instance, [14, 15] adopted personalized DP to location and communication graphs, respectively. Varying the privacy level across inputs also makes sense in "continuous" scenarios, where the neighborhood relationship between two datasets is not binary, but quantified. This is, for example, the case for *geo-indistinguishability* [16], where two datasets D_1 and D_2 are considered "r-neighbors" if the only different record between D_1 and D_2 are at a distance r of each other, and the ε grows linearly with r.

Both personalization and neighborhood can be naturally captured together via distance functions. In [17], the authors introduce $d_{\mathcal{D}}$-*privacy*, in which the function $d_{\mathcal{D}}$ takes both datasets as input and returns the corresponding maximal privacy loss (the σ) depending on the difference between the two datasets.

Definition 4 [$d_{\mathcal{D}}$-*privacy* [17]] Let $d_{\mathcal{D}} : \mathcal{D}^2 \to \mathbb{R}_\infty$. A privacy mechanism $\mathcal{M}$ satisfies $d_{\mathcal{D}}$-privacy ($d_{\mathcal{D}}$-Pr) if for all pairs of datasets $D_1, D_2 \mathcal{M}(D_1) \approx_{d(D_1, D_2)} \mathcal{M}(D_2)$.

When $d_{\mathcal{D}}$ is proportional to the Hamiltonian difference between datasets, this is equivalent to ε-DP. In the original definition, the authors impose that $d_{\mathcal{D}}$ is symmetric, but this condition can also be relaxed to allow $d_{\mathcal{D}}$-privacy to extend definitions like one-sided DP.

Equivalent definitions of $d_{\mathcal{D}}$-privacy also appeared in [18] as *l-privacy*, in [19] as *spatial-personalized DP*, and in [20] as *extended DP*. Several other definitions, such as *weighted DP* [21], *smooth DP* [22][1] and *earth mover's privacy* [24], can be seen as particular instantiations of $d_{\mathcal{D}}$-privacy for specific functions d measuring the distance between datasets. This is also the case for some definitions tailored for location privacy, like *geo-graph-indistinguishability* [25, 26], which specifically applies to network graphs.

Random DP can also be combined with changing the neighborhood definition: in [27], the authors define *DP on a δ-location set* ,[2], for which the neighborhood is defined by a set of "plausible" locations around the true location of a user. A notable definition using the same combination of dimensions is *distributional privacy*[3] introduced in [30, 31]: It combines random DP (for a large family of distributions) and free lunch privacy.

Definition 5 [(ε, γ)-*distributional privacy* [30, 31]] An algorithm $\mathcal{M}$ satisfies (ε, γ)-distributional privacy (DlPr) if for any distribution π over possible tuples, if $D_1, D_2 \in \mathcal{D}$ are picked by randomly drawing a fixed number n of elements from π without replacement, then with probability at least $1 - \gamma$ over the choice of D_1 and D_2, $\mathcal{M}(D_1) \approx_{\varepsilon} \mathcal{M}(D_2)$.

Interestingly, this definition captures an intuition similar to the DP modifications in Chap. 8: the adversary can only learn properties of the data-generating distribution, but not about particular samples (except with probability lower than γ).

Combination with Q

Different risk models, like the definitions in Chap. 3, are also compatible with varying the privacy parameters across inputs. For example, in [32], the author proposes *endogeneous DP*, which includes an additive δ term in personalized DP. Similarly, *pseudo-metric DP*, defined in [33], is a combination of $d_{\mathcal{D}}$-privacy and (ε, δ)-DP, while *extended divergence DP*, defined in [34], is a combination of $d_{\mathcal{D}}$-privacy and divergence DP.

Randomly limiting the scope of the definition can also be combined with ideas from the previous chapters. For example, in [35], the authors introduce *weak Bayesian DP*, which combines random DP and approximate DP. In [23], the authors introduced *Smoothed DP*[4] which require (ε, δ)-indistinguishability to hold for all the expected dataset from a set of distributions. Similarly, in [36, 37], the authors introduce *on average KL privacy* and *average leave-one-out KL stability*, respectively, both using KL-divergence as quantification metric, but only requires the property to hold for an "average dataset."

In [35, 38], the authors introduce *Bayesian DP*[5] and *privacy at risk*, respectively; both definitions combine random DP with probabilistic DP, with slightly different

---

[1] Distinct from *Smoothed DP* [23] introduced later in this chapter.

[2] Distinct from *DP on r-location set* [28], which we mention in Chap. 4.

[3] Another definition with the same name is introduced in [29], we mention it in Chap. 4.

[4] Distinct from *Smooth DP* [22] introduced earlier in this chapter.

[5] There are two other notions with the same name: introduced in [39, 40], we mention them in Chaps. 4 and 6, respectively.

approaches: the former quantifies over all possible datasets and changes one fixed record randomly, while the latter selects both datasets randomly, conditioned on these datasets being neighbors.

In [41], the authors further generalize the intuition from generic DP (introduced in Chap. 4) by generalizing the indistinguishability condition entirely. The resulting definition is also called generic DP.

Definition 6 [$(\mathcal{R}, M)$-*generic differential privacy* [41, 42]] A privacy mechanism $\mathcal{M}$ satisfies $(\mathcal{R}, M)$-generic DP (GcDP) if for all measurable sets $S \subseteq \mathcal{O}$ and for all $(D_1, D_2) \in \mathcal{R}$:

$$M_{D_1,D_2}(\mathbb{P}[\mathcal{M}(D_1) \in S]) \geq \mathbb{P}[\mathcal{M}(D_2) \in S]$$
$$M_{D_1,D_2}(\mathbb{P}[\mathcal{M}(D_1) \notin S]) \geq \mathbb{P}[\mathcal{M}(D_2) \notin S]$$

where $M_{D_1,D_2} : [0, 1] \to [0, 1]$ is a concave function continuous on $(0, 1)$ such as $M_{D_1,D_2}(1) = 1$.

The privacy relation $\mathcal{R}$ is still the generalization of neighborhood, and the privacy predicate is the generalization of the ε-indistinguishability to arbitrary functions. In particular, it can encompass all variants of described in Chap. 3 in addition to the ones in this chapter: For example, if $M_{D_1,D_2}(x) = \min\left(1, xe^\varepsilon + \delta, 1 - (1 - x - \delta)e^{-\varepsilon}\right)$ holds for all D_1 and D_2, then this is equivalent to (ε, δ)-DP. This definition was an attempt at finding the most generic definition that still satisfies privacy axioms: Another extension defined in the same work, *abstract DP* is even more generic, but no longer satisfies the privacy axioms.

Definitions in this chapter are particularly used in the context of local DP (detailed in Chap. 11), and in particular for applications to location privacy: Various metrics have been discussed to quantify how indistinguishable different places should be to provide users of a local DP mechanism with meaningful privacy protection.

References

1. Niknami, N., Abadi, M., Deldar, F.: Spatialpdp: a personalized differentially private mechanism for range counting queries over spatial databases. In: 2014 4th International eConference on Computer and Knowledge Engineering (ICCKE). IEEE (2014)
2. Jorgensen, Z., Yu, T., Cormode, G.: Conservative or liberal? Personalized differential privacy. In: 2015 IEEE 31st International Conference on Data Engineering (ICDE). IEEE (2015)
3. Ebadi, H., Sands, D., Schneider, G.: Differential privacy: now it's getting personal. ACM, In Acm Sigplan Notices (2015)
4. Ghosh, A., Roth, A.: Selling privacy at auction. Games Econ. Behav. (2015)
5. Liu, Z., Wang, Y.-X., Smola, A.: Fast differentially private matrix factorization. In: Proceedings of the 9th ACM Conference on Recommender Systems. ACM (2015)
6. Alaggan, M., Gambs, S., Kermarrec, A.-M.: Heterogeneous differential privacy. J. Privacy Confidential. 7(2), 127–158 (2016)
7. Lui, E., Pass, R.: Outlier privacy. In: Theory of Cryptography Conference. Springer (2015)

8. Gu, X., Li, M., Xiong, L., Cao, Y.: Providing input-discriminative protection for local differential privacy. In: 2020 IEEE 36th International Conference on Data Engineering (ICDE), pp. 505–516. IEEE (2020)
9. Kartal, H.B., Liu, X., Li, X.-B.: Differential privacy for the vast majority. ACM Trans. Manag. Inf. Syst. (TMIS) (2019)
10. Hall, R., Wasserman, L., Rinaldo, A.: Random differential privacy. J. Privacy Confidential. **4**(2) (2013)
11. Hall, R.: New statistical applications for differential privacy. Ph.D. thesis, Carnegie Mellon (2012)
12. McClure, D.R.: Relaxations of differential privacy and risk/utility evaluations of synthetic data and fidelity measures. Ph.D. thesis, Duke University (2015)
13. Dixit, K., Jha, M., Raskhodnikova, S., Thakurta, A.: Testing lipschitz property over product distribution and its applications to statistical data privacy. In: Theory of Cryptography—Lecture Notes in Computer Science (2013)
14. Deldar, F., Abadi, M.: Pldp-td: Personalized-location differentially private data analysis on trajectory databases. Pervasive Mobile Comput. (2018)
15. Seres, I., Pejó, B., Burcsi, P.: The effect of false positives: why fuzzy message detection leads to fuzzy privacy guarantees? (2021) arXiv preprint arXiv:2109.06576
16. Andrés, M.E., Bordenabe, N.E., Chatzikokolakis, K., Palamidessi, C.: Geo-indistinguishability: differential privacy for location-based systems. In: Proceedings of the 2013 ACM SIGSAC Conference on Computer & communications security. ACM (2013)
17. Chatzikokolakis, K., Andrés, M.E., Bordenabe, N.E., Palamidessi, C.: Broadening the scope of differential privacy using metrics. In: International Symposium on Privacy Enhancing Technologies Symposium. Springer (2013)
18. ElSalamouny, E., Gambs, S.: Differential privacy models for location-based services. Trans. Data Privacy (2016)
19. Niknami, N., Abadi, M., Deldar, F.: A fully spatial personalized differentially private mechanism to provide non-uniform privacy guarantees for spatial databases. Inf. Syst. **92**, 101526 (2020)
20. Kawamoto, Y and Takao Murakami. Local obfuscation mechanisms for hiding probability distributions. In: European Symposium on Research in Computer Security. Springer (2019)
21. Proserpio, D., Goldberg, S., McSherry, F.: Calibrating data to sensitivity in private data analysis: a platform for differentially-private analysis of weighted datasets. Proceedings of the VLDB Endowment (2014)
22. Barber, R.F., Duchi, J.C.: Privacy and statistical risk: formalisms and minimax bounds (2014). arXiv preprint arXiv:1412.4451
23. Liu, A., Xia, L.: Smoothed differential privacy (2021). arXiv preprint arXiv:2107.01559
24. Fernandes, N., Dras, M., McIver, A.: Generalised differential privacy for text document processing. In: International Conference on Principles of Security and Trust. Springer (2019)
25. Takagi, S., Cao, Y., Asano, Y., Yoshikawa, M.: Geo-graph-indistinguishability: protecting location privacy for lbs over road networks. In: IFIP Annual Conference on Data and Applications Security and Privacy. Springer (2019)
26. Takagi, S., Cao, Y., Asano, Y., Yoshikawa, M.: Geo-graph-indistinguishability: location privacy on road networks based on differential privacy (2020). arXiv preprint arXiv:2010.13449
27. Xiao, Y., Xiong, L.: Protecting locations with differential privacy under temporal correlations. In: Proceedings of the 22nd ACM SIGSAC Conference on Computer and Communications Security. ACM (2015)
28. Chen, Z., Bao, X., Ying, Z., Liu, X., Zhong, H.: Differentially private location protection with continuous time stamps for Vanets. In: International Conference on Algorithms and Architectures for Parallel Processing. Springer (2018)
29. Zhou, S., Ligett, K., Wasserman, L.: Differential privacy with compression. In: IEEE International Symposium on Information Theory: ISIT 2009. IEEE (2009)
30. Roth, A.: New algorithms for preserving differential privacy. Microsoft Res. (2010)

31. Blum, A., Ligett, K., Roth, A.: A learning theory approach to noninteractive database privacy. J. ACM (JACM) (2013)
32. Krehbiel, S.: Choosing epsilon for privacy as a service. Proceedings on Privacy Enhancing Technologies (2019)
33. Dimitrakakis, C., Nelson, B., Mitrokotsa, A., Rubinstein, B, et al.: Bayesian differential privacy through posterior sampling (2013). arXiv preprint arXiv:1306.1066
34. Kawamoto, Y., Murakami, T.: Local distribution obfuscation via probability coupling. In: 2019 57th Annual Allerton Conference on Communication, Control, and Computing (Allerton). IEEE (2019)
35. Triastcyn, A., Faltings, B.: Bayesian differential privacy for machine learning. In: International Conference on Machine Learning, pp. 9583–9592. PMLR (2020)
36. Wang, Y.-X., Lei, J., Fienberg, S.E.: On-average kl-privacy and its equivalence to generalization for max-entropy mechanisms. In: International Conference on Privacy in Statistical Databases. Springer (2016)
37. Feldman, V., Steinke, T.: Calibrating noise to variance in adaptive data analysis. In: Proceedings of Machine Learning Research (2018)
38. Dandekar, A., Basu, D., Bressan, S.: Differential privacy at risk: Bridging randomness and privacy budget. Proc. Privacy Enhanc. Technol. 1, 64–84 (2021)
39. Yang, B., Sato, I., Nakagawa, H.: Bayesian differential privacy on correlated data. In: Proceedings of the 2015 ACM SIGMOD International Conference on Management of Data. ACM (2015)
40. Leung, S., Lui, E.: Bayesian mechanism design with efficiency, privacy, and approximate truthfulness. In: International Workshop on Internet and Network Economics. Springer (2012)
41. Kifer, D., Lin, B.-R.: Towards an axiomatization of statistical privacy and utility. In: Proceedings of the Twenty-ninth ACM SIGMOD-SIGACT-SIGART Symposium on Principles of Database Systems. ACM (2010)
42. Kifer, D., Lin, B.-R.: An axiomatic view of statistical privacy and utility. J. Privacy Confidential. (2012)

Chapter 6
Background Knowledge (B)

In DP, the attacker is implicitly assumed to have full knowledge of the dataset: Their only uncertainty is whether the target belongs in the dataset or not. This implicit assumption is also present for the definitions of the previous dimensions: Indeed, the attacker has to distinguish between two "fixed" datasets D_1 and D_2. The only source of randomness in ε-indistinguishability comes from the mechanism itself. In many cases, this assumption is unrealistic, and it is natural to consider weaker adversaries, who do not have full background knowledge. One of the main motivations to do so is to use significantly less noise in the mechanism.

The typical way to represent this uncertainty formally is to assume that the input data comes from a certain probability distribution (named "data evolution scenario" in [1]): the randomness of this distribution models the attacker's uncertainty. Informally, the more random this probability distribution is, the less knowledge the attacker has. However, the definition that follows depends whether DP is considered with the associative or the causal view. In the associative view, the sensitive property changes before the data is generated: It conditions the data-generating probability distribution. In the causal view, however, the sensitive property is only changed after the data is generated. The two options lead to very distinct definitions.

6.1 Conditioning on the Sensitive Property

Using a probability distribution to generate the input data means that the ε-indistinguishability property cannot be expressed between two fixed datasets. Instead, one natural way to express it is to condition this distribution on some sensitive property. The corresponding notion, *noiseless privacy*[1] was first introduced in [3] and formalized in [4].

---

[1] Another definition with the same name is introduced in [2], we mention it in Chap. 11.

B. Pejó and D. Desfontaines, *Guide to Differential Privacy Modifications*,
SpringerBriefs in Computer Science,
https://doi.org/10.1007/978-3-030-96398-9_6

Definition 1 $((\Theta, \varepsilon)$-*noiseless privacy* [4]] Given a family Θ of probability distribution on $\mathcal{D}$, a mechanism $\mathcal{M}$ is (Θ, ε)-noiseless private (NPr) if for all $\theta \in \Theta$, all i and all $t, t' \in \mathcal{T}$:

$$\mathcal{M}(D)_{|D \sim \theta, D(i)=t} \approx_{\varepsilon} \mathcal{M}(D)_{|D \sim \theta, D(i)=t'}$$

In the original definition, the "auxiliary knowledge" of the attacker is explicitly pointed out in an additional parameter. In the case where this idea is not combined with an additive term δ as in Chap. 3, this is not necessary [5], so we omitted it here. This definition follows naturally from considering the associative view of DP with the strong adversary assumption and attempting to relax this assumption.

6.2 Removing the Effect of Correlations

In [6], however, the authors argue that in the presence of correlations in the data noiseless privacy can be too strong, and make it impossible to learn global properties of the data. Indeed, if one record can have an arbitrarily large influence on the rest of the data, conditioning on the value of this record can lead to very distinguishable outputs even if the mechanism only depends on global properties of the data. To fix this problem, they propose *distributional DP*, an alternative definition that that only conditions the data-generating distribution on one possible value of the target record and quantifies the information leakage from the mechanism[2]. In [5], the authors show that this creates definitional issues in the presence of background knowledge and introduce *causal DP*, to capture the same intuition without encountering the same problems.

Definition 2 $[(\Theta, \varepsilon)$-*causal differential privacy* [5]] Given a family Θ of probability distributions on $\mathcal{D}$, a mechanism $\mathcal{M}$ satisfies (Θ, ε)-causal DP (CaDP) if for all probability distributions $\theta \in \Theta$, for all i and all $t, t' \in \mathcal{T}$:

$$\mathcal{M}(D)_{|D \sim \theta, D(i)=t} \approx_{\varepsilon} \mathcal{M}(D_{i \to t'})_{|D \sim \theta, D(i)=t}$$

where $D_{i \to t'}$ is the dataset obtained by changing the ith record of D into t'.

In this definition, one record is changed after the dataset has been generated, so it does not affect other records through dependence relationships. These dependence relationships are the only difference between noiseless privacy and causal DP: When each record is independent of all others, this definition is equivalent to noiseless privacy.

---

[2] Note that the original formalization used in [6] was more abstract, and uses a simulator, similarly to variants introduced in Chap. 8.

6.3 Multidimensional Definitions

Limiting the background knowledge of an attacker is orthogonal to the dimensions introduced previously: One can modify the risk model, introduce different neighborhood definitions, or even vary the privacy parameters across the protected properties along with limiting the attacker background knowledge.

Combination with Q
Modifying the risk model while limiting the attacker's background knowledge has interesting consequences. In [5], the authors show that two options are possible: Either consider the background knowledge as additional information given to the attacker or let the attacker "influence" the background knowledge. This distinction between an "active" and a "passive" attacker does not matter if only the worst-case scenario is considered, like in noiseless privacy. However, under different risk models, such as allowing a small probability of error, they lead to two different definitions.

Both of these definitions use an adapted version of the PLRV $\mathcal{L}_{i \leftarrow (\cdot)/i \leftarrow (\cdot)}^{\mathcal{M}, \theta}$ [5] which explicitly models the attacker background knowledge: The data-generating distribution not only generates a dataset D but also some auxiliary knowledge B, with values in a set $\mathcal{B}$. Using this formalization can then be used to adapt noiseless privacy to a risk model similar to (ε, δ)-DP, in the case of an active or a passive attacker. The active variant, *active partial knowledge differential privacy*, quantifies over all possible values of the background knowledge. It was first introduced in [4, 6] as *noiseless privacy* and reformulated in [5] to clarify that it implicitly assumes an active attacker.

Definition 3 [$(\Theta, \varepsilon, \delta)$-*active partial knowledge DP* [4–6] Given a family Θ of probability distribution on $\mathcal{D} \times \mathcal{B}$, a mechanism $\mathcal{M}$ is $(\Theta, \varepsilon, \delta)$-active partial knowledge DP (APKDP) if for all $\theta \in \Theta$, all indices i, all $t, t' \in \mathcal{T}$, and all possible values $\hat{B}$ of the background knowledge:

$$\mathbb{E}_{(D,B) \sim \theta_{|D(i)=t, B=\hat{B}}, O \sim \mathcal{M}(D)} \left[\max \left(0, 1 - e^{\varepsilon - \mathcal{L}_{i \leftarrow t/i \leftarrow t'}^{\mathcal{M}, \theta}(O, \hat{B})} \right) \right] \leq \delta$$

One specialization of this definition is *DP under sampling* [7], which mandates DP to be satisfied after a random sampling is applied to the dataset. The authors use this definition to show that applying k-anonymity to a randomly sampled dataset provides DP, but this definition could also be used on its own, to model the attacker's uncertainty using a randomly sampled distribution.

The second definition, *passive partial knowledge differential privacy* [5], is strictly weaker: It models a passive attacker, who cannot choose their background knowledge and thus cannot influence the data. In this context, δ does not only apply to the output of the mechanism, but also to the value of the background knowledge.

Definition 4 [$(\Theta, \varepsilon, \delta)$-*passive partial knowledge DP* [5]] Given a family Θ of probability distribution on $\mathcal{D} \times \mathcal{B}$, a mechanism $\mathcal{M}$ is $(\Theta, \varepsilon, \delta)$-passive partial knowledge DP (PPKDP) if for all $\theta \in \Theta$, all indices i, and all $t, t' \in \mathcal{T}$:

$$\mathbb{E}_{(D,B)\sim\theta_{|D(i)=t},O\sim\mathcal{M}(D)}\left[\max\left(0, 1 - e^{\varepsilon-\mathcal{L}^{\mathcal{M},\theta}_{i\leftarrow t/i\leftarrow t'}(O,B)}\right)\right] \le \delta$$

Causal DP can also be adapted to a risk model similar to (ε, δ)-DP: In [8], authors introduce a similar notion called *inherit DP*, with the small difference that the second dataset is obtained by removing one record from the first dataset, instead of replacing it; and (ε, δ)-indistinguishability is used. The authors also define *empirical DP*[3], which is identical, except the empirical distribution is used instead of the actual data distribution, in context where the latter is unknown. In both cases, the influence of δ on the attacker model is unclear.

Combination with N and V

Modifying the neighborhood definition is simpler: It is clearly orthogonal to the dimensions introduced in this chapter. In all definitions of this chapter so far, the two possibilities between which the adversary must distinguish are similar to bounded DP. This can easily be changed to choose other properties to protect from the attacker. This is done in *pufferfish privacy* [1].

Definition 5 [$(\Theta, \Phi, \varepsilon)$-*pufferfish privacy* [1]] Given a family of probability distributions Θ on $\mathcal{D}$, and a family of pairs of predicates Φ on datasets, a mechanism $\mathcal{M}$ verifies $(\Theta, \Phi, \varepsilon)$-pufferfish privacy (PFPr) if for all distributions $\theta \in \Theta$ and all pairs of predicates $(\phi_1, \phi_2) \in \Phi$:

$$\mathcal{M}(D)_{|D\sim\theta,\phi_1(D)} \approx_\varepsilon \mathcal{M}(D)_{|D\sim\theta,\phi_2(D)}$$

Pufferfish privacy extends the concept of neighboring datasets to neighboring "distributions" of datasets; starting with a set of data-generating distributions, then conditioning them on sensitive attributes. The result compares pairs of distributions encompasses noiseless privacy, as well as other notions. For example, it captures *bayesian DP*,[4] introduced in [12], in which neighboring records have up to k fixed elements in common and all other elements are generated randomly from a distribution π.

The same idea can be formalized by comparing pairs of distributions directly. This is done in [13, 14] via *distribution privacy*. The two formalisms are equivalent: An arbitrary pair of distributions can be seen as a single distribution, conditioned on the value of a secret parameter. Distribution privacy was instantiated in [15] via *profile-based DP*, in which the attacker tries to distinguish between different probabilistic user profiles. A similar idea was proposed in [16] as *robust privacy*, which uses lossy Wasserstein distance over the corresponding outputs to define the neighborhood of the inputs.

Further relaxations encompassing the introduced dimensions are *probabilistic distribution privacy* [14], a combination of distribution privacy and probabilistic DP, *extended distribution privacy* [14], a combination of distribution privacy and

---

[3] Another definition with the same name is introduced in [9], we mention it in Chap. 11.

[4] There are two other notions with the same name: Introduced in [10, 11], we mention them in Chaps. 4 and 5, respectively.

d_D-privacy, *divergence distribution privacy* [17], a combination of distribution privacy, *extended divergence distribution privacy* [17], a combination of the latter two definitions, and finally *divergence distribution privacy with auxiliary inputs* [17] which considers the setting where the attacker might not know the input probability distribution perfectly.

Definitions of this section are an active area of research; a typical question is to quantify in which conditions deterministic mechanisms can provide some level privacy. However, they are not used a lot in practice, likely because of their fragility: If the assumptions about the attacker's limited background knowledge are wrong in practice, then the definitions do not provide any guarantee of protection.

References

1. Kifer, D., Machanavajjhala, A.: A rigorous and customizable framework for privacy. In: Proceedings of the 31st ACM SIGMOD-SIGACT-SIGAI Symposium on Principles of Database Systems. ACM (2012)
2. Farokhi, F.: Noiseless privacy: definition, guarantees, and applications. IEEE Trans. Big Data (2021)
3. Duan, Y.: Privacy without noise. In: Proceedings of the 18th ACM Conference on Information and Knowledge Management. ACM (2009)
4. Bhaskar, R., Bhowmick, A., Goyal, V., Laxman, S., Thakurta, A.: Noiseless database privacy. In: International Conference on the Theory and Application of Cryptology and Information Security. Springer (2011)
5. Desfontaines, D., Mohammadi, E., Krahmer, E., Basin, D.: Differential privacy with partial knowledge. arXiv preprint arXiv:1905.00650 (2019)
6. Bassily, R., Groce, A., Katz, J., Smith, A.: Coupled-worlds privacy: exploiting adversarial uncertainty in statistical data privacy. In: 2013 IEEE 54th Annual Symposium on Foundations of Computer Science (FOCS). IEEE (2013)
7. Li, N., Qardaji, W., Su, D.: On sampling, anonymization, and differential privacy or, k-anonymization meets differential privacy (2012)
8. Burchard, P., Daoud, A.: Empirical differential privacy. arXiv preprint arXiv:1910.12820 (2019)
9. Abowd, J.M., Schneider, M.J., Vilhuber, L.: Differential privacy applications to bayesian and linear mixed model estimation. J. Privacy Confidential. (2013)
10. Yang, B., Sato, I., Nakagawa, H.: Bayesian differential privacy on correlated data. In: Proceedings of the 2015 ACM SIGMOD International Conference on Management of Data. ACM (2015)
11. Triastcyn, A., Faltings, B.: Bayesian differential privacy for machine learning. In: International Conference on Machine Learning, pp. 9583–9592. PMLR (2020)
12. Leung, S., Lui, E.: Bayesian mechanism design with efficiency, privacy, and approximate truthfulness. In: International Workshop on Internet and Network Economics. Springer (2012)
13. Jelasity, M., Birman, K.P.: Distributional differential privacy for large-scale smart metering. In: Proceedings of the 2nd ACM Workshop on Information Hiding and Multimedia Security. ACM (2014)
14. Kawamoto, Y., Murakami, T.: Local obfuscation mechanisms for hiding probability distributions. In: European Symposium on Research in Computer Security. Springer (2019)
15. Geumlek, J., Chaudhuri, K.: Profile-based privacy for locally private computations. In: 2019 IEEE International Symposium on Information Theory (ISIT), pp. 537–541. IEEE (2019)

16. Bansal, A., Chunduru, R., Data, D., Prabhakaran, M.: Robustness and flexibility, Extending the foundations of differential privacy (2019)
17. Kawamoto, Y., Murakami, T.: Local distribution obfuscation via probability coupling. In: 2019 57th Annual Allerton Conference on Communication, Control, and Computing (Allerton). IEEE (2019)

Chapter 7
Change in Formalism (F)

The definition of DP using ε-indistinguishability compares the distribution of outputs given two neighboring inputs. This is not the only way to capture the idea that an attacker should not be able to gain too much information on the dataset. Other formalisms have been proposed, which model the attacker more explicitly.

One such formalism reformulates DP in terms of hypothesis testing by limiting the type I and the type II error of the hypothesis that the output O of a mechanism originates from D_1 (instead of D_2). Other formalisms model the attacker explicitly, by formalizing their prior belief as a probability distribution over all possible datasets. This can be done in two distinct ways. Some variants consider a specific prior (or family of possible priors) of the attacker, implicitly assuming a limited background knowledge, like in Chap. 6. We show that these variants can be interpreted as changing the prior–posterior bounds of the attacker. Finally, rather than comparing prior and posterior, a third formalism compares two possible posteriors, quantifying over all possible priors.

Definitions in this chapter provide a deeper understanding of the guarantees given by DP, and some of them lead to tighter and simpler theorems on DP, like composition or amplification results.

7.1 Hypothesis Testing Interpretation

DP can be interpreted in terms of hypothesis testing [1, 2]. In this context, an adversary who wants to know whether the output O of a mechanism originates from D_1 (the null hypothesis) or D_2 (the alternative hypothesis). Calling S the rejection region, the probability of false alarm (type I error), when the null hypothesis is true but rejected, is $\mathbb{P}_{FA} = \mathbb{P}[\mathcal{M}(D_1) \in S]$. The probability of missed detection (type II error), when the null hypothesis is false but retained, is $\mathbb{P}_{MD} = \mathbb{P}[\mathcal{M}(D_2) \in \mathcal{O}/S]$.

B. Pejó and D. Desfontaines, *Guide to Differential Privacy Modifications*,
SpringerBriefs in Computer Science,
https://doi.org/10.1007/978-3-030-96398-9_7

It is possible to use these probabilities to reformulate DP:

$$\varepsilon - DP \Leftrightarrow \mathbb{P}_{FA} + e^{\varepsilon}\mathbb{P}_{MD} \geq 1$$
$$e^{\varepsilon}\mathbb{P}_{FA} + \mathbb{P}_{MD} \geq 1 \quad \text{for all} \ \ S \subseteq \mathcal{O}$$
$$\varepsilon - DP \Leftrightarrow \mathbb{P}_{FA} + \mathbb{P}_{MD} \geq \frac{2}{1 + e^{\varepsilon}}$$
$$(\varepsilon, \delta) - DP \Leftrightarrow (\mathbb{P}_{FA}, \mathbb{P}_{MD}) = \{(\alpha, \beta) \in [0, 1] \times [0, 1] :$$
$$(1 - \alpha \leq e^{\varepsilon}\beta + \delta)\}$$

This hypotheses testing interpretation was used in [3] to define f-DP, which avoids difficulties associated with divergence based relaxations. Specifically, its composition theorem is lossless as it provides a computationally tractable tool for analytically approximating the privacy loss. As such, the connection between f-DP (ε, δ)-DP and Rényi DP is highlighted in [4] and in [5] via the *sensitivity index*.

Definition 7.1 (*f-differential privacy* [3]). Let $f : [0, 1] \to [0, 1]$ be a convex, continuous, and non-increasing function such that for all $x \in [0, 1]$, $f(x) \leq 1 - x$. A privacy mechanism $\mathcal{M}$ satisfies f-DP if for all neighboring D_1, D_2 and all $x \in [0, 1]$:

$$\inf_{S} \{1 - \mathbb{P}[\mathcal{M}(D_2) \in S] \,|\, \mathbb{P}[\mathcal{M}(D_1) \in S] \leq x\} \geq f(x)$$

Here, S is the rejection region, and the infimum is the trade-off function between $\mathcal{M}(D_1)$ and $\mathcal{M}(D_2)$. The authors also introduce *Gaussian DP* as an instance of f-DP, which tightly bounds from below the hardness of determining whether an individual's data was used in a computation than telling apart two shifted Gauss distributions. Besides, *weak* and *strong federated f-DP* [6] are also defined that adopts the definition for federated learning [7]. They describe the privacy guarantee against an individual and a group of adversaries, respectively.

7.2   Prior–Posterior Bounds

Differential privacy can be interpreted as giving a bound on the posterior of a Bayesian attacker as a function of their prior. This is exactly the case in *indistinguishable privacy*, an equivalent reformulation of ε-DP defined in [8]: suppose that the attacker is trying to distinguish between two options $D = D_1$ and $D = D_2$, where D_1 corresponds to the option "$t \in D$" and D_2 to "$t \notin D$." Initially, they associate a certain prior probability $\mathbb{P}[t \in D]$ to the first option. When they observe the output of the algorithm, this becomes the posterior probability $\mathbb{P}[t \in D | \mathcal{M}(D) = O]$. Combining the definition of ε-DP and the Bayes theorem, we have[1]:

---

[1] Note that the original formalization used in [8] was more abstract, and it used polynomially bounded adversaries what we introduce in Chap. 9.

$$\frac{\mathbb{P}[t \in D|\mathcal{M}(D) = O]}{\mathbb{P}[t \notin D|\mathcal{M}(D) = O]} \leq e^{\varepsilon} \cdot \frac{\mathbb{P}[t \in D]}{\mathbb{P}[t \notin D]} \Rightarrow$$

$$\mathbb{P}[t \in D|\mathcal{M}(D) = O] \leq \frac{e^{\varepsilon} \cdot \mathbb{P}[t \in D]}{1 + (e^{\varepsilon} - 1)\mathbb{P}[t \in D]}$$

A similar, symmetric lower bound can be obtained. Hence, DP can be interpreted as bounding the posterior level of certainty of a Bayesian attacker as a function of its prior. We visualize these bounds on the top left of Fig. 7.1.

Some variants of DP use this idea in their formalism, rather than obtaining the posterior bound as a corollary to the classical DP definition. For example, *positive membership privacy* [9] requires that the posterior does not increase too much compared to the prior. Like noiseless privacy, it assumes an attacker with limited background knowledge.

Definition 7.2 ((Θ, ε)-*positive membership privacy* [9]). A privacy mechanism $\mathcal{M}$ provides (Θ, ε)-positive membership privacy (PMPr) if for any distribution $\theta \in \Theta$, any record $t \in D$ and any $S \subseteq O$:

$$\mathbb{P}_{D \sim \theta}[t \in D|\mathcal{M}(D) \in S] \leq e^{\varepsilon}\mathbb{P}_{D \sim \theta}[t \in D]$$
$$\mathbb{P}_{D \sim \theta}[t \notin D|\mathcal{M}(D) \in S] \geq e^{-\varepsilon}\mathbb{P}_{D \sim \theta}[t \notin D]$$

We visualize this bound on the top right of Fig. 7.1. Note that this definition is "asymmetric": The posterior is bounded from above, but not from below. In the same paper, the authors also define *negative membership privacy*, which provides the symmetric lower bound, and *membership privacy*,[2] which is the conjunction of positive and negative membership privacy. Bounding the ratio between prior and posterior by e^{ε} is also done in the context of location privacy: in [11, 12], authors define ε-*DP location obfuscation* and $P_{\%}$-*DP*, respectively, which formalizes the same intuition as membership privacy.

A previous attempt at formalizing the same idea was presented in [13] as *adversarial privacy*. This definition is similar to positive membership privacy, except only the first relation is used, and there is a small additive δ as in approximate DP. We visualize the corresponding bounds on the bottom left of Fig. 7.1. Adversarial privacy (without δ) was also redefined in [14] as *information privacy*.[3]

Definition 7.3 (($\Theta, \varepsilon, \delta$)-*adversarial privacy* [13]). An algorithm $\mathcal{M}$ is ($\Theta, \varepsilon, \delta$)-adversarial private (AdvPr) if for all $S \subseteq O$, tuples t, and distributions $\theta \in \Theta$:

$$\mathbb{P}_{D \sim \theta}[t \in D|\mathcal{M}(D) \in S] \leq e^{\varepsilon} \cdot \mathbb{P}_{D \sim \theta}[t \in D] + \delta$$

---

[2] Another definition with the same name is introduced in [10], we mention it in Chap. 11.

[3] Another definition with the same name is introduced in [15], we mention it later in this chapter.

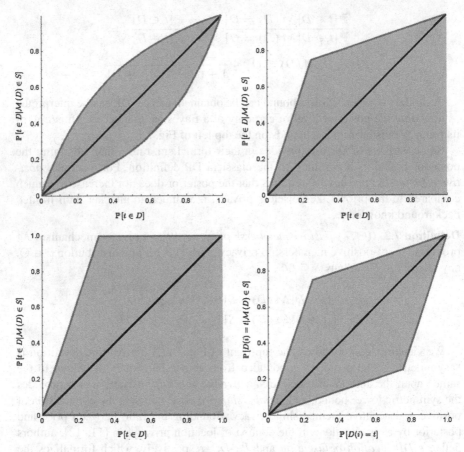

Fig. 7.1 From top left to bottom right, using $\varepsilon = \ln 3$: posterior-prior bounds in DP, positive membership privacy, adversarial privacy (with $\delta = 0.05$), and a posteriori noiseless privacy

Finally, *a posteriori noiseless privacy* is a similar variant of noiseless privacy introduced in [16]; the corresponding bounds can be seen on the bottom right figure of Fig. 7.1.

Definition 7.4 ((Θ, ε)-*a posteriori noiseless privacy* [16]). A mechanism $\mathcal{M}$ is said to be (Θ, ε)-a posteriori noiseless private (ANPr) if for all $\theta \in \Theta$, all $S \subseteq \mathcal{O}$, and all i:

$$D(i)_{|D\sim\theta,\mathcal{M}(D)\in S} \approx_\varepsilon D(i)_{|D\sim\theta}$$

7.3 Comparing Two Posteriors

In [17, 18], the authors propose an approach that captures an intuitive idea proposed in [19]: "any conclusions drawn from the output of a private algorithm must be similar whether or not an individual's data is present in the input or not." They define *semantic privacy*: Instead of comparing the posterior with the prior belief like in DP, this bounds the difference between two posterior belief distributions, depending on which dataset was secretly chosen. The distance chosen to represent the idea that those two posterior belief distributions are close is the statistical distance. One important difference between the definitions in the previous subsection is that semantic privacy quantifies over all possible priors: Like in DP, the attacker is assumed to have arbitrary background knowledge.

Definition 7.5 (*ε-semantic privacy* [17, 18]). A mechanism $\mathcal{M}$ is ε-semantically private (SemPr) if for any distribution over datasets θ, any index i, any $S \subseteq \mathcal{O}$, and any set of datasets $X \subseteq \mathcal{D}$:

$$\left| \mathbb{P}_{D \sim \theta} \left[D \in X \mid \mathcal{M}(D) \in S \right] - \mathbb{P}_{D \sim \theta} \left[D \in X \mid \mathcal{M}(D_{-i}) \in S \right] \right| \leq \varepsilon$$

A couple of other definitions also compare posteriors directly: *Inferential privacy* [20] is a reformulation of noiseless privacy, and *range-bounded privacy* [21] requires that two different values of the PLRV are close to each other (instead of being between centered around zero like in ε-DP).

7.4 Multidimensional Definitions

This dimension could be combined with other dimensions fairly easily; several DP modifications from this chapter does belong to multiple dimensions, but to introduce the concept used within this chapter, we overlooked these details. Definitions that limit the background knowledge of the adversary explicitly formulate it as a probability distribution. As such, they are natural candidates for Bayesian reformulations. In [14], the authors introduce *identity DP*, which is an equivalent Bayesian reformulation of noiseless privacy. Another example is *inference-based causal DP* [22], similar to a posteriori noiseless DP, except it uses causal DP instead of noiseless DP.

The authors of semantic privacy also combined it with probabilistic DP, and simply called it (ε, δ)-*semantic privacy*. Further, it is possible to consider different definitions of neighborhood. In [15], authors introduce *information privacy*,[4] which can be seen as a posteriori noiseless privacy combined with free lunch privacy: Rather than only considering the knowledge gain of the adversary on one particular user, it considers its knowledge gain about any possible group of values of the dataset.

---

[4] Another definition with the same name is introduced in [14], we mention it earlier in this chapter.

Definition 7.6 $((\Theta, \varepsilon)$-*information privacy* [15]). A mechanism $\mathcal{M}$ satisfies (Θ, ε)-information privacy (InfPr) if for all probability distributions $\theta \in \Theta$, all $D \in \mathcal{D}$ and all $O \in \mathcal{O}$, $D_{|D \sim \theta} \approx_{\varepsilon} D_{|D \sim \theta, \mathcal{M}(D) = O}$.

Apart from the hypothesis testing reformulations, that can be used to improve composition and amplification results, the definitions in this chapter mostly appear in theoretical research papers to provide a deeper understanding of guarantees offered by DP and its alternatives.

References

1. Wasserman, L., Zhou, S.: A statistical framework for differential privacy. J. Am. Stat. Assoc. (2010)
2. Kairouz, P., Oh, S., Viswanath, P.: The composition theorem for differential privacy. IEEE Trans. Inf. Theory (2017)
3. Dong, J., Roth, A., Su, W.: Gaussian differential privacy. J. R. Stat. Soc. (2021)
4. Asoodeh, S., Liao, J., Calmon, F.P., Kosut, O., Sankar, L.: Three variants of differential privacy: lossless conversion and applications. IEEE J. Sel. Areas Inf. Theory **2**(1), 208–222 (2021)
5. Kaissis, G., Knolle, M., Jungmann, F., Ziller, A., Usynin, D., Rueckert, D.: A unified interpretation of the gaussian mechanism for differential privacy through the sensitivity index. *arXiv preprint* arXiv:2109.10528 (2021)
6. Zheng, Q., Chen, S., Long, Q., Su, W.: Federated f-differential privacy. In: International Conference on Artificial Intelligence and Statistics, pp. 2251–2259. PMLR (2021)
7. Brendan McMahan, H., et al.: Advances and open problems in federated learning. Found. Trends Mach. Learn. **14**(1) (2021)
8. Liu, J., Xiong, L., Luo, J.: Semantic security: privacy definitions revisited. Trans. Data Privacy (2013)
9. Li, N., Qardaji, W., Su, D., Wu, Y., Yang, W.: Membership privacy: a unifying framework for privacy definitions. In: Proceedings of the 2013 ACM SIGSAC Conference on Computer & Communications Security. ACM (2013)
10. Sablayrolles, A., Douze, M., Schmid, C., Ollivier, Y., Jégou, H.: White-box vs black-box: Bayes optimal strategies for membership inference. In: International Conference on Machine Learning, pp. 5558–5567. PMLR (2019)
11. Dong, K., Guo, T., Ye, H., Li, X., Ling, Z.: On the limitations of existing notions of location privacy. Future Gener. Comput. Syst. (2018)
12. Dong, K., Tao, Z., Xia, X., Chen, Z., Yang, M.: Preserving privacy for discrete location information. In: 2021 IEEE 24th International Conference on Computer Supported Cooperative Work in Design (CSCWD), pp. 360–365. IEEE (2021)
13. Rastogi, V., Hay, M., Miklau, G., Suciu, D.: Relationship privacy: output perturbation for queries with joins. In: Proceedings of the Twenty-Eighth ACM SIGMOD-SIGACT-SIGART Symposium on Principles of Database Systems
14. Wu, G., Xia, X., He, Y.: Information theory of data privacy. *arXiv preprint* arXiv:1703.07474 (2017)
15. du Pin Calmon, F., Fawaz, N.: Privacy against statistical inference. In: 2012 50th Annual Allerton Conference on Communication, Control, and Computing (Allerton). IEEE (2012)

16. Bhaskar, R., Bhowmick, A., Goyal, V., Laxman, S., Thakurta, A.: Noiseless database privacy. In: International Conference on the Theory and Application of Cryptology and Information Security. Springer (2011)
17. Ganta, S.R., Kasiviswanathan, S.P., Smith, A.: Composition attacks and auxiliary information in data privacy. In: Proceedings of the 14th ACM SIGKDD International Conference on Knowledge Discovery and Data Mining. ACM (2008)
18. Kasiviswanathan, S.P., Smith, A.: On the 'semantics' of differential privacy: a bayesian formulation. J. Privacy Confid. (2014)
19. Dwork, C.: Differential privacy. In: Proceedings of the 33rd International Conference on Automata, Languages and Programming. ACM (2006)
20. Ghosh, A., Kleinberg, R.: Inferential privacy guarantees for differentially private mechanisms. In: 8th Innovations in Theoretical Computer Science Conference (ITCS 2017). Schloss Dagstuhl-Leibniz-Zentrum fuer Informatik (2017)
21. Durfee, D., Rogers, R.M.: Practical differentially private top-k selection with pay-what-you-get composition. In: Advances in Neural Information Processing Systems (2019)
22. Desfontaines, D., Mohammadi, E., Krahmer, E., Basin, D.: Differential privacy with partial knowledge. *arXiv preprint* arXiv:1905.00650 (2019)

Chapter 8
Knowledge Gain Relativization (R)

A differentially private mechanism does not reveal more than a bounded amount of probabilistic information about a user. This view does not explicitly take into account other ways information can leak, like side-channel functions or knowledge about the structure of a social network. We found two approaches that attempt to include such auxiliary functions in DP variants. One possibility is to weaken DP by allowing or disregarding a certain amount of leakage; another option is to explicitly forbid the mechanism to reveal more than another function, considered to be safe for release.

8.1 Auxiliary Leakage Functions

In [1], authors define *bounded leakage DP*, which quantifies the privacy that is maintained by a mechanism despite bounded, additional leakage of information by some leakage function. Interestingly, this leakage function P shares the randomness of the privacy mechanism: It can, for example, capture side-channel leakage from the mechanism's execution. In the formal definition of this DP variant, the randomness is "explicit": The privacy mechanism and the leakage take the random bits $r \in \{0, 1\}^*$ as an additional parameter. If there is no leakage, this is simply (ε, δ)-DP, and if the privacy mechanism is independent from the leakage function, it is strictly weaker than that.

Definition 8.1 ((P, ε)-*bounded leakage DP* [1]) Let $P : \mathcal{D} \times \{0, 1\}^*$ be a leakage function. A privacy mechanism $\mathcal{M}$ is (P, ε)-bounded leakage differentially private (BLDP) if for all pairs of neighboring datasets D_1 and D_2, all outputs O_P of P such that $0 \neq \mathbb{P}[P(D_1, r) = O_P]$ and $\mathbb{P}[P(D_2, r) = O_P] \neq 0$, and all sets of outputs $S \subseteq \mathcal{O}$:

$$\mathbb{P}[\mathcal{M}(D_1, r) \in S \mid P(D_1, r) = O_P] \leq$$
$$e^\varepsilon \cdot \mathbb{P}[\mathcal{M}(D_2, r) \in S \mid P(D_2, r) = O_P]$$

where the randomness is taken over the random bits r.

© The Author(s), under exclusive license to Springer Nature Switzerland AG 2022   51
B. Pejó and D. Desfontaines, *Guide to Differential Privacy Modifications*,
SpringerBriefs in Computer Science,
https://doi.org/10.1007/978-3-030-96398-9_8

8.2   Zero-knowledge Proofs

When using the associative interpretation with the independence assumption, it is
unclear how to adapt DP to correlated datasets like social networks: Data about
someone's friends might reveal sensitive information about this person. The causal
interpretation of DP does not suffer from this problem, but how to adapt the associative view to such correlated contexts? Changing the definition of the neighborhood
is one possibility (see Chap. 4), but it requires knowing in advance the exact impact
of someone on other records. A more robust option is to impose that the information
released does not contain more information than the result of some predefined algorithms on the data, without the individual in question. The method for formalizing
this intuition borrows ideas from zero-knowledge proofs [2].

Instead of imposing that the result of the mechanism is roughly "the same" on
neighboring datasets D_1 and D_2, the intuition is to impose that the result of the mechanism on D_1 can be "simulated" using only some information about D_2. The corresponding definition, called *zero-knowledge privacy* and introduced in [3], captures
the idea that the mechanism does not leak more information on a given target than
a certain class of aggregate metrics. This class, called "model of aggregate information" is formalized by a family of (possibly randomized) family of algorithms Agg.
This is yet another way to formalize the intuition that DP protects against attackers
who have full background knowledge.

Definition 8.2 ((Agg, ε)-*zero-knowledge privacy* [3]). Let Agg be a family of (possibly randomized) algorithms agg. A privacy mechanism $\mathcal{M}$ is (Agg, ε)-zero-
knowledge private (ZKPr) if there exists an algorithm agg $\in$ Agg and a simulator
Sim such as for all datasets D and indices i, $\mathcal{M}(D) \approx_\varepsilon$ Sim (agg (D_{-i})).

Another approach is to ignore some leakage instead of limiting it. This is done in
subspace DP [4], which require DP to holds for a subspace within the projection of
the range of $\mathcal{M}$. Furthermore, *induced subspace DP* [4] is also defined which ensures
that the output of $\mathcal{M}$ does meet the invariant-linear external constraints. Essentially,
they say for a mechanism to satisfy subspace DP, the function $D \rightarrow f(\mathcal{M}(D))$ must
be DP for some function f.

8.3   Multidimensional Definitions

Similarly to Chap. 7, some of the already detailed notions does belong to other dimensions as well. Using a simulator allows making statements of the type "this mechanism does not leak more information on a given target than a certain class of aggregate
metrics." Similarly to noiseless privacy, it is possible to explicitly limit the attacker's
background knowledge using a data-generating probability distribution, as well as
vary the neighborhood definitions to protect other types of information than the presence and characteristics of individuals. This is done in [5] as *coupled-worlds privacy*,
where a family of functions priv represents the protected attribute.

Definition 8.3 ((Θ, Γ, ε)-*coupled-worlds privacy* [5]). Let Γ be a family of pairs of functions (agg, priv). A mechanism $\mathcal{M}$ satisfies (Θ, Γ, ε)-coupled-worlds privacy if there is a simulator Sim such that for all distributions $\theta \in \Theta$, all (agg, priv) $\in \Gamma$, and all possible values p:

$$\mathcal{M}(D)_{|D\sim\theta,\mathrm{priv}(D)=p} \approx_{\varepsilon} \mathrm{Sim}(\mathrm{agg}(D))_{|D\sim\theta,\mathrm{priv}(D)=p}$$

A special case of coupled-worlds privacy is also introduced in [5] as *distributional DP*, already mentioned in Chapter 6: Each function priv captures the value of a single record, and the corresponding function agg outputs all other records.

Coupled-worlds privacy is a good example of combining variants from different dimensions: It changes several aspects of the original definition according to from N, B and R. Moreover, Q and F can easily be integrated with this definition by using (ε, δ)-indistinguishability with a Bayesian reformulation. This is done explicitly in *inference-based coupled-worlds privacy* [5]; the same paper also introduces *inference-based distributional DP*.

Definition 8.4 ((Θ, Γ, ε, δ)-*inference-based coupled-worlds privacy* [5]). Given a family Θ of probability distributions on $\mathcal{D} \times \mathcal{B}$, and a family Γ of pairs of functions (agg, priv), a mechanism $\mathcal{M}$ satisfies (Θ, Γ, ε, δ)-inference-based coupled-worlds privacy (IBCWPr) if there is a simulator Sim such that for all distributions $\theta \in \Theta$, and all (agg, priv) $\in \Gamma$:

$$\mathrm{priv}(D)_{|(D,B)\sim\theta,\mathcal{M}(D)=O,B=\hat{B}} \approx_{(\varepsilon,\delta)} \mathrm{priv}(D)_{|(D,B)\sim\theta,\mathrm{Sim}(\mathrm{agg}(D))=O,B=\hat{B}}$$

with probability at least $1 - \delta$ over the choice of O and $\hat{B}$.

Random DP was also combined with an idea similar to ZKPr: in [6], the authors introduce *typical stability*, which combines random DP with approximate DP, except that rather using (ε, δ)-indistinguishability between two outputs of the mechanism, it uses a simulator that only knows data-generating distribution.

Definition 8.5 ((Θ, γ, ε, δ)-*typical stability* [6]). Given a family Θ of probability distributions on $\mathcal{D}$, a mechanism $\mathcal{M}$ satisfies (Θ, γ, ε, δ)-typical stability (TySt) if for all distributions $\theta \in \Theta$, there is a simulator Sim such that with probability at least $1 - \gamma$ over the choice of $D \sim \theta$, $\mathcal{M}(D) \approx_{\varepsilon,\delta} \mathrm{Sim}(\theta)$.

In the same paper, the authors introduce a variant of the same definition with the same name, which compares two outputs of the mechanism; this is essentially a combination between distributional Pr and (ε, δ)-DP.

We did not find any evidence that the variants and extensions of this section are used outside of theoretical papers exploring the guarantees they provide.

References

1. Ligett, K., Peale, C., Reingold, O.: Bounded-leakage differential privacy. In: 1st Symposium on Foundations of Responsible Computing (FORC 2020). Schloss Dagstuhl-Leibniz-Zentrum für Informatik (2020)
2. Goldwasser, S., Micali, S., Rackoff, C.: The knowledge complexity of interactive proof systems. SIAM J. Comput. (1989)
3. Gehrke, J., Lui, E., Pass, R.: Towards privacy for social networks: a zero-knowledge based definition of privacy. In: Theory of Cryptography Conference. Springer (2011)
4. Gao, J., Gong, R., Yu, F.-Y.: Subspace differential privacy. *arXiv preprint* arXiv:2108.11527 (2021)
5. Bassily, R., Groce, A., Katz, J., Smith, A.: Coupled-worlds privacy: exploiting adversarial uncertainty in statistical data privacy. In: 2013 IEEE 54th Annual Symposium on Foundations of Computer Science (FOCS). IEEE (2013)
6. Bassily, R., Freund, Y.: Typical stability. *arXiv preprint* arXiv:1604.03336 (2016)

Chapter 9
Computational Power (C)

The ε-indistinguishability property in DP is "information-theoretic": The attacker is implicitly assumed to have infinite computing power. This is unrealistic in practice, so it is natural to consider definitions where the attacker only has polynomial computing power. Changing this assumption leads to weaker data privacy definitions. In [1], two approaches have been proposed to formalize this idea: Either modeling the distinguisher explicitly as a polynomial Turing machine, or allowing a mechanism not to be technically differentially private, as long as one cannot distinguish it from a truly differentially private one.

Using a polynomial distinguisher on the output

The attacker is not explicit in the formalization of DP based on ε-indistinguishability. It is possible change the definition to make this attacker explicit: Model it as a "distinguisher," who tries to guess whether a given output O comes from a dataset D_1 or its neighbor D_2. In doing so, it becomes straightforward to require this attacker to be computationally bounded: Simply model it as a probabilistic polynomial-time Turing machine. In [1], the authors introduce IndCDP, short for *indistinguishability-based computational DP*.

Definition 9.1 (ε_κ-*IndCDP* [1]). A family $(\mathcal{M}_\kappa)_{\kappa \in \mathbb{N}}$ of privacy mechanisms $\mathcal{M}_\kappa$ provides ε_κ-IndCDP if there exists a negligible function neg such that for all nonuniform probabilistic polynomial-time Turing machines Ω (the distinguisher), all polynomials $p(\cdot)$, all sufficiently large $\kappa \in \mathbb{N}$, and all datasets $D_1, D_2 \in \mathcal{D}$ of size at most $p(\kappa)$ that differ only one one record:

$$\mathbb{P}\left[\Omega(\mathcal{M}(D_1)) = 1\right] \leq e^{\varepsilon_\kappa} \cdot \mathbb{P}\left[\Omega(\mathcal{M}(D_2)) = 1\right] + \mathsf{neg}(\kappa)$$

where neg is a function that converges to zero asymptotically faster than the reciprocal of any polynomial.

This definition can also be expressed using *differential indistinguishability*, a notion defined in [2] that adapts indistinguishability to a polynomially bounded attacker.

B. Pejó and D. Desfontaines, *Guide to Differential Privacy Modifications*,
SpringerBriefs in Computer Science,
https://doi.org/10.1007/978-3-030-96398-9_9

Using a polynomial distinguisher on the mechanism

Another natural option is to require that the mechanism "looks like" a truly differentially private mechanism, at least to a computationally bounded distinguisher. In [1], the authors introduce SimCDP, short for *simulation-based computational DP*.

Definition 9.2 (ε_κ-*SimCDP* [1]). A family $(\mathcal{M}_\kappa)_{\kappa \in \mathbb{N}}$ of privacy mechanisms $\mathcal{M}_\kappa$ provides ε_κ-SimCDP if there exists a family $(\mathcal{M}'_\kappa)_{\kappa \in \mathbb{N}}$ of ε_κ-DP and a negligible function neg such that for all nonuniform probabilistic polynomial-time Turing machines Ω, all polynomials $p(\cdot)$, all sufficiently large $\kappa \in \mathbb{N}$, and all datasets $D \in \mathcal{D}$ of size at most $p(\kappa)$:

$$\mathbb{P}[\Omega(\mathcal{M}(D)) = 1] - \mathbb{P}\left[\Omega(\mathcal{M}'(D)) = 1\right] \le \mathsf{neg}(\kappa)$$

where neg is a function that converges to zero asymptotically faster than the reciprocal of any polynomial.

9.1   Multidimensional Definitions

IndCDP has been adapted to different settings, and extended to arbitrary neighborhood relationships. In *output constrained DP*, introduced in [3], the setting is a two-party computation, each party can have its own set of privacy parameters, and the neighborhood relationship is determined by a function f. The authors also propose an instance of it, called *DP for Record Linkage*, that uses for a specific function f that captures the need to protect nonmatching records during the execution of a private record linkage protocol.

Some DP variants which explicitly model an adversary with a simulator can relatively easily be adapted to model a computationally bounded adversary, simply by imposing that the simulator must be polynomial. This is done explicitly in [4], where the authors define *computational zero-knowledge privacy*.

Further, although we have not seen this done in practice in existing literature, the idea behind SimCDP can in principle be adapted to any other definition. Limiting the computational power of the attacker is a reasonable assumption, but for a large class of queries, it cannot provide significant benefits over classical DP in the typical client–server setting [5]. Thus, existing work using it focuses on multiparty settings [6].

References

1. Mironov, I., Pandey, O., Reingold, O., Vadhan, S.: Computational differential privacy. In: Advances in Cryptology-CRYPTO 2009. Springer (2009)
2. Backes, M., Kate, A., Meiser, S., Ruffing, T.: Differential indistinguishability for cryptography with (bounded) weak sources. Grande Region Security and Reliability Day (GRSRD) (2014)

3. He, X., Machanavajjhala, A., Flynn, C., Srivastava, D.: Composing differential privacy and secure computation: a case study on scaling private record linkage. In: Proceedings of the 2017 ACM SIGSAC Conference on Computer and Communications Security. ACM (2017)
4. Gehrke, J., Lui, E., Pass, R.: Towards privacy for social networks: a zero-knowledge based definition of privacy. In: Theory of Cryptography Conference. Springer (2011)
5. Groce, A., Katz, J., Yerukhimovich, A.: Limits of computational differential privacy in the client/server setting. In: Theory of Cryptography Conference. Springer (2011)
6. Bater, J., He, X., Ehrich, W., Machanavajjhala, A., Rogers, J.: Shrinkwrap: efficient sql query processing in differentially private data federations. In: Proceedings of the VLDB Endowment (2018)

Chapter 10
Summarizing Table

In this chapter, we summarize the results from the seven dimensions into tables where we list the known relations and show the properties with either referring to the original proof or creating a novel one. In Tables 10.1, 10.2, 10.3, 10.4, 10.5, 10.6, and 10.7, we list the differential privacy modifications introduced in this book. For each, we specify their name, parameters, and where they were introduced (column 1), which dimensions they belong to (column 2), which axioms they satisfy (column 3, post-processing on the left and convexity on the right), whether they are composable (column 4), and how they relate to other DP notions (column 5). We do not list definitions whose only difference is that they apply DP to other types of input, like those from Sect. 4.3, or geolocation-specific definitions. Furthermore, we only include the most popular modifications corresponding to the same change, and we exclude variants which merely adds an additive δ to another definition.

10.1 Proofs of Properties

Axioms

Proposition 10.1 *All instantiations of DivDP satisfy both privacy axioms. In particular, approximate DP, MIDP, KLPr, RenDP, and zCoDP satisfy both axioms.*

Proof The post-processing axiom follows directly from the monotonicity property of the f-divergence. The convexity axiom follows directly from the joint convexity property of the f-divergence. $\qquad\square$

© The Author(s), under exclusive license to Springer Nature Switzerland AG 2022
B. Pejó and D. Desfontaines, *Guide to Differential Privacy Modifications*,
SpringerBriefs in Computer Science,
https://doi.org/10.1007/978-3-030-96398-9_10

Table 10.1 Summary of DP modifications representing the main options in dimension Q

Name and References	Dimension	Axioms		Composition	Relations
		Postprocessing	Convexity		
(ε, δ)-approximate DP [1]	Q	✓[a]	✓[a]	✓✓	(ε, δ)-**DP** $\supset^\curlyvee \varepsilon$-DP
(ε, δ)-probabilistic DP [2]	Q	✗[j]	✗[b]	✓✓	(ε, δ)-**DP** $\sim (\varepsilon, \delta)$-**ProDP**
$(\varepsilon, \delta_a, \delta_p)$-Relaxed DP [3]	Q	✗[j]	✗[b]	✓✓	(ε, δ_p)-**ProDP** $\subset^\curlyvee (\varepsilon, \delta_a, \delta_p)$-**RelDP** ; (ε, δ_a)-DP $\subset^\curlyvee (\varepsilon, \delta_a, \delta_p)$-**RelDP**
ε-Kullback-Leiber Pr [4]	Q	✓[a]	✓[a]	✓✓	(ε, δ)-DP $\prec \varepsilon$-**KLPr** $\prec \varepsilon$-DP
(α, ε)-Rényi DP [5]	Q	✓[a]	✓[a]	✓✓	ε-**KLPr** $\subset^\curlyvee (\alpha, \varepsilon)$-**RényiDP** $\supset^\curlyvee \varepsilon$-DP
(μ, τ)-mean concentrated DP [6]	Q	✗[j]	?	✓✓	(ε, δ)-DP $\prec (\mu, \tau)$-**mCoDP** $\prec \varepsilon$-DP
(ξ, ρ)-zero concentrated DP [7]	Q	✓[a]	✓[a]	✓✓	(ξ, ρ)-**zCoDP** $\sim (\mu, \tau)$-mCoDP
(ξ, ρ, δ)-approximate CoDP [7]	Q	✗[a]	?	✓✓	(ε, δ)-DP $\succ (\xi, \rho, \delta)$-**ACoDP** $\supset^\curlyvee (\xi, \rho)$-zCoDP
(ξ, ρ, ω)-bounded CoDP [7]	Q	✓[a]	✓[a]	✓✓	(ξ, ρ, ω)-**BCoDP** $\supset^\curlyvee (\xi, \rho)$-zCoDP
(η, τ)-truncated CoDP [8]	Q	✓[a]	✓[a]	✓✓	(η, τ)-**TCoDP** [8] $\sim \varepsilon$-DP

Table 10.1 (continued)

Name and References	Dimension	Axioms		Composition	Relations
		Postprocessing	Convexity		
(ρ, ω)-truncated CoDP [9]	Q	✓a	✓a	✓j	(ρ, ω)-**TCoDP** [9] $\subseteq^\vee (\xi, \rho, \omega)$-**bCoDP**
(f, ε)-divergence DP [10]	Q	✓a	✓a	?	(f, ε)-**DivDP** $\supseteq$most def. in Q
(f_k, ε)-divergence DP [11]	Q	✓a	✓a	?	(f_k, ε)-**kDivDP** $\subseteq (f, \varepsilon)$-DivDP
(H, f, ε)-capacity bounded DP [12]	Q	✓a	✓a	?	(H, f, ε)-**CBDP** $\subseteq^\vee (f, \varepsilon)$-DivDP

[a]See Proposition 10.1.

[b]See Proposition 10.2.

[c]See Proposition 10.3.

[d]See Proposition 10.4.

[e]See Proposition 10.5.

[f]See Proposition 10.6.

[g]See Proposition 10.7.

[h]See Proposition 10.8.

[i]Follows directly from its equivalence with ε-DP.

[j]A proof appears in the paper introducing the definition.

[k]A proof for a restricted scenario appears in the paper introducing the definition.

[l]This claim appears in [5], its proof is in the unpublished full version.

Table 10.2 Summary of DP modifications representing the main options in dimension $\mathbb{N}$

Name and References	Dimensions	Axioms		Composition	Relations
		Postprocessing	Convexity		
ε-unbounded DP [13]	$\mathbb{N}$	$\checkmark$	$\checkmark$	$\checkmark^g$	ε-DP $\sim\varepsilon$-**uBoDP** $\subset^\sim (c, \varepsilon)$-GrDP
ε-bounded DP [13]	$\mathbb{N}$	$\checkmark$	$\checkmark$	$\checkmark^g$	ε-**BoDP** $\prec\varepsilon$-DP
(P, ε)-one-sided DP [14]	$\mathbb{N}$	$\checkmark$	$\checkmark$	$\checkmark^g$	(P, ε)-**OnSDP** $\supset^\prec\varepsilon$-BoDP
(P, ε)-asymmetric DP [15]	$\mathbb{N}$	$\checkmark$	$\checkmark$	$\checkmark^g$	(P, ε)-**AsDP** $\supset^\prec\varepsilon$-uBoDP
ε-client DP [16]	$\mathbb{N}$	$\checkmark$	$\checkmark$	$\checkmark^g$	ε-**ClDP** $\succ\varepsilon$-DP
ε-element DP [17]	$\mathbb{N}$	$\checkmark$	$\checkmark$	$\checkmark^g$	ε-**ClDP** $\succ\varepsilon$-**ElDP** $\succ\varepsilon$-DP
(c, ε)-group DP [18]	$\mathbb{N}$	$\checkmark$	$\checkmark$	$\checkmark^g$	(c, ε)-**GrDP** $\supset^\sim\varepsilon$-DP
(R, c, ε)-dependent DP [19]	$\mathbb{N}$	$\checkmark$	$\checkmark$	$\checkmark^g$	(R, c, ε)-**DepDP** $\supset(c, \varepsilon)$-GrDP
$(\mathcal{A}, \varepsilon)$-bayesian DP [20]	$\mathbb{N}$	$\checkmark$	$\checkmark$	$\checkmark^g$	$(\mathcal{A}, \varepsilon)$-**BayDP** [20] $\supset(R, c, \varepsilon)$-DepDP
$(\mathcal{A}, \varepsilon)$-correlated DP [21, 22]	$\mathbb{N}$	$\checkmark$	$\checkmark$	$\checkmark^g$	$(\mathcal{A}, \varepsilon)$-**CorDP** $\subset (\mathcal{A}, \varepsilon)$-**BayDP** [20]
$(\mathcal{A}, \varepsilon)$-prior DP [23]	$\mathbb{N}$	$\checkmark$	$\checkmark$	$\checkmark^g$	$(\mathcal{A}, \varepsilon)$-**PriDP** $\supset(\mathcal{A}, \varepsilon)$-**BayDP** [20]
ε-free lunch Pr [13]	$\mathbb{N}$	$\checkmark$	$\checkmark$	$\checkmark^g$	ε-**FLPr** $\succ$ all def. in $\mathbb{N}$
(D, ε)-individual DP [24]	$\mathbb{N}$	$\checkmark$	$\checkmark$	$\checkmark^g$	(D, ε)-**IndDP** $\prec\varepsilon$-DP
(D, t, ε)-per-instance DP [25]	$\mathbb{N}$	$\checkmark$	$\checkmark$	$\checkmark^g$	(D, t, ε)-**PIDP** $\prec(D, \varepsilon)$-IndDP
$(\mathcal{R}, \varepsilon)$-generic DP [13, 26]	$\mathbb{N}$	$\checkmark$	$\checkmark$	$\checkmark^g$	$(\mathcal{R}, \varepsilon)$-**GcDP** [13] $\supset$ most def. in $\mathbb{N}$
(d, Δ, ε)-constrained DP [27]	$\mathbb{N}$	$\checkmark$	$\checkmark$	$\checkmark^g$	(d, Δ, ε)-**ConsDP** $\sim(\mathcal{R}, \varepsilon)$-GcDP

Table 10.2 (continued)

Name and References	Dimensions	Axioms Postprocessing	Convexity	Composition	Relations
$(d, \Delta, S_D, \varepsilon)$-distributional Pr [27]	N	✓i	✓i	✓g	$(d, \Delta, S_D, \varepsilon)$-**DIPr** [27] $\subset (\mathcal{R}, \varepsilon)$-GcDP
(f, ε)-sensitivity-induced DP [28]	N	✓i	✓i	✓g	ε-**SIDP** $\subset (\mathcal{R}, \varepsilon)$-GcDP
$(\mathcal{I}_Q, \varepsilon)$-induced-neighbors DP [13]	N	✓i	✓i	✓g	$(\mathcal{I}_Q, \varepsilon)$-**INDP** $\subset (\mathcal{R}, \varepsilon)$-GcDP
$(G, \mathcal{I}_Q, \varepsilon)$-blowfish Pr [29]	N	✓i	✓i	✓g	$(G, \mathcal{I}_Q, \varepsilon)$-**BFPr** $\subset (\mathcal{R}, \varepsilon)$-GcDP

a See Proposition 10.1.
b See Proposition 10.2.
c See Proposition 10.3.
d See Proposition 10.4.
e See Proposition 10.5.
f See Proposition 10.6.
g See Proposition 10.7.
h See Proposition 10.8.
i Follows directly from its equivalence with ε-DP.
j A proof appears in the paper introducing the definition.
k A proof for a restricted scenario appears in the paper introducing the definition.
l This claim appears in [5], its proof is in the unpublished full version.

Table 10.3 Summary of DP modifications representing the main options in dimension V

Name and References	Dimensions	Axioms		Composition	Relations
		Postprocessing	Convexity		
Ψ-personalized DP [30]	V	$\checkmark^c$	$\checkmark^c$	$\checkmark^g$	Ψ-**PerDP** $\supset \varepsilon$-DP
Ψ-tailored DP [31]	V	$\checkmark^c$	$\checkmark^c$	$\checkmark^g$	Ψ-**TailDP** $\supset \Psi$-PerDP
$(\Psi, \overline{\varepsilon})$-input-discriminative DP [32]	V	$\checkmark^c$	$\checkmark^c$	$\checkmark^g$	Ψ-**IDDP** $\supset \Psi$-PerDP
$\varepsilon(\cdot)$-outlier Pr [31]	V	$\checkmark^c$	$\checkmark^c$	$\checkmark^g$	$\varepsilon(\cdot)$-**OutPr** $\subset \Psi$-TailDP
(ε, p, r)-Pareto DP [31]	V	$\checkmark^c$	$\checkmark^c$	$\checkmark^g$	(ε, p, r)-**ParDP** $\subset \Psi$-TailDP
$(\pi, \gamma, \varepsilon)$-random DP [33]	V	?	χ^d	$\checkmark^j$	$(\pi, \gamma, \varepsilon)$-**RanDP** $\supset^{\prec} \varepsilon$-DP
$d_{\mathcal{D}}$-Pr [34]	N, V	$\checkmark^c$	$\checkmark^c$	$\checkmark^g$	ε-DP $\subset d_{\mathcal{D}}$-**Pr**
$(d_{\mathcal{D}}, \varepsilon)$-smooth DP [10]	N, V	$\checkmark^c$	$\checkmark^c$	$\checkmark^g$	$(d_{\mathcal{D}}, \varepsilon)$-**SmDP** $\sim d_{\mathcal{D}}$-Pr
(ε, γ)-distributional Pr [27, 35]	N, V	?	?	?	ε-FLPr $\subset (\varepsilon, \gamma)$-**DIPr** [35, 36]
$(\pi, \varepsilon, \delta)$-weak Bayesian DP [37]	Q, V	$\checkmark^j$	?	$\checkmark^g$	(ε, δ)-DP $\succ (\pi, \varepsilon, \delta)$-**WBDP** $\prec (\pi, \gamma, \varepsilon)$-RanDP
(Θ, ε)-on average KL Pr [38]	Q, V	$\checkmark^j$	?	$?^k$	ε-KLPr $\succ (\Theta, \varepsilon)$-**avgKLPr** $\prec (\pi, \gamma, \varepsilon)$-RanDP
$(\pi, \varepsilon, \delta)$-Bayesian DP [37]	Q, V	$\checkmark^j$	χ^d	$\checkmark^g$	(ε, δ)-ProDP $\succ (\pi, \varepsilon, \delta)$-**BayDP** [37] $(\pi, \gamma, \varepsilon)$-RanDP $\succ (\pi, \varepsilon, \delta)$-**BayDP** [37]
$(d_{\mathcal{D}}, \varepsilon, \delta)$-pseudo-metric DP [39]	Q, N, V	?	?	$\checkmark^j$	(ε, δ)-DP $\subset (d_{\mathcal{D}}, \varepsilon, \delta)$-**PsDP** $\supset^{\prec} d_{\mathcal{D}}$-Pr

Table 10.3 (continued)

Name and References	Dimensions	Axioms Postprocessing	Convexity	Composition	Relations
(f, d, ε)-extended divergence DP [40]	Q, N, V	$\checkmark^c$	$\checkmark^c$	?	d_D-Pr $\subset (f, d, \varepsilon)$-**EDivDP** $\supset (f, \varepsilon)$-**Div DP**
$(\mathcal{R}, M)$-generic DP [41]	Q, N, V	$\checkmark^j$	$\checkmark^j$	?	$(\mathcal{R}, M)$-**GcDP** [41] $\supset (\varepsilon, \delta)$-DP
$(\mathcal{R}, q)$-abstract DP [41]	Q, N, V	χ^j	χ^j	?	$(\mathcal{R}, q)$-**AbsDP** $\supset (\mathcal{R}, M)$-**GcDP** [41]

a See Proposition 10.1.
b See Proposition 10.2.
c See Proposition 10.3.
d See Proposition 10.4.
e See Proposition 10.5.
f See Proposition 10.6.
g See Proposition 10.7.
h See Proposition 10.8.
i Follows directly from its equivalence with ε-DP.
j A proof appears in the paper introducing the definition.
k A proof for a restricted scenario appears in the paper introducing the definition.
l This claim appears in [5], its proof is in the unpublished full version.

Table 10.4 Summary of DP modifications representing the main options in dimension B

Name and References	Dimensions	Axioms		Composition	Relations
		Postprocessing	Convexity		
(Θ, ε)-noiseless Pr [42]	B	✓j	✓j	χ^h	ε-DP $\supset^{\prec}(\Theta, \varepsilon)$-**NPr**
(Θ, ε)-causal DP [43]	B	✓j	✓j	χ^h	(Θ, ε)-**CausDP** $\supset^{\prec}\varepsilon$-DP
(β, ε)-DP under sampling [44]	Q, B	✓j	✓j	χ^h	(Θ, ε)-NPr $\supset(\beta, \varepsilon)$-**SamDP** $\supset^{\prec}\varepsilon$-DP
$(\Theta, \varepsilon, \delta)$-active PK DP [43]	Q, B	✓j	✓j	χ^h	$(\Theta, \varepsilon, \delta)$-**APKDP** $\supset^{\prec}(\Theta, \varepsilon)$-NPr
$(\Theta, \varepsilon, \delta)$-passive PK DP [43]	Q, B	✓j	✓j	χ^h	$(\Theta, \varepsilon, \delta)$-APKDP $\succ(\Theta, \varepsilon, \delta)$-**PPKDP** (Θ, ε)-NPr $\subset^{\prec}(\Theta, \varepsilon, \delta)$-**PPKDP**
$(\Theta, \Phi, \varepsilon)$-pufferfish Pr [45]	N, B	✓j	✓j	χ^h	(Θ, ε)-NPr $\subset(\Theta, \Phi, \varepsilon)$-**PFPr** $\supset(\mathcal{R}, \varepsilon)$-GcDP
(π, k, ε)-Bayesian DP [46]	N, B	✓j	✓j	χ^h	BayDP [46] $\subset(\Theta, \Phi, \varepsilon)$-PFPr
$(\Theta, \varepsilon, \delta)$-distribution Pr [47, 48]	Q, N, B	✓c	✓c	χ^h	$(\Theta, \varepsilon, \delta)$-**DnPr** $\supset(\Theta, \varepsilon, \delta)$-APKDP
$(\Theta, \varepsilon, \delta)$-profile-based DP [49]	Q, N, B	✓c	✓c	χ^h	$(\Theta, \varepsilon, \delta)$-**PBDP** $\subset(\Theta, \varepsilon, \delta)$-DnPr

Table 10.4 (continued)

Name and References	Dimensions	Axioms Postprocessing	Axioms Convexity	Composition	Relations
$(\Theta, \varepsilon, \delta)$-probabilistic DnPr [48]	Q, N, B	✗ʲ	✗ᵇ	✗ʰ	ε-ProDP $\subset (\Theta, \varepsilon, \delta)$-**PDnPr** $\supset (\Theta, \varepsilon)$-DnPr
(f, Θ, ε)-divergence DnPr [40]	Q, N, B	✓ᶜ	✓ᶜ	✗ʰ	(f, ε)-DP $\subset (f, \Theta, \varepsilon)$-**DDnPr** $\supset (\Theta, \varepsilon)$-DnPr
(d, Θ, ε)-extended DnPr [48]	N, V, B	✓ᶜ	✓ᶜ	✗ʰ	d_D-Pr $\subset (d, \Theta, \varepsilon)$-**EDnPr** $\supset (\Theta, \varepsilon)$-DnPr
$(d, f, \Theta, \varepsilon)$-ext. div. DnPr [40]	Q, N, V, B	✓ᶜ	✓ᶜ	✗ʰ	(f, Θ, ε)-DDPr $\subset (d, f, \Theta, \varepsilon)$-**EDDnPr** (d, Θ, ε)-EDnPr $\subset (d, f, \Theta, \varepsilon)$-**EDDnPr**

ᵃSee Proposition 10.1.
ᵇSee Proposition 10.2.
ᶜSee Proposition 10.3.
ᵈSee Proposition 10.4.
ᵉSee Proposition 10.5.
ᶠSee Proposition 10.6.
ᵍSee Proposition 10.7.
ʰSee Proposition 10.8.
ⁱFollows directly from its equivalence with ε-DP.
ʲA proof appears in the paper introducing the definition.
ᵏA proof for a restricted scenario appears in the paper introducing the definition.
ˡThis claim appears in [5], its proof is in the unpublished full version.

Table 10.5 Summary of DP modifications representing the main options in dimension F

Name and References	Dimensions	Axioms		Composition	Relations
		Postprocessing	Convexity		
ε-indistinguishable Pr [50]	F	$\checkmark^i$	$\checkmark^i$	$\checkmark^i$	ε-**IndPr** $\sim \varepsilon$-DP
ε-semantic Pr [51, 52]	F'	?	?	?	ε-**SemPr** $\sim \varepsilon$-DP
ε-range-bounded Pr [53]	F	?	?	?	ε-**RBPr** $\sim \varepsilon$-DP
f-DP [54]	Q, F	$\checkmark^j$	?	$\checkmark^j$	f-**DP** $\supset (\varepsilon, \delta)$-DP
Gaussian DP [54]	Q, F	$\checkmark^j$	?	$\checkmark^j$	**GaussDP** $\subset f$-DP
weak-Federated f-DP [55]	Q, F	$\checkmark^j$	?	$\checkmark^j$	f-**wFDP** $\subset$ GaussDP
strong-Federated f-DP [55]	Q, F	$\checkmark^j$	?	$\checkmark^j$	f-wFDP $\prec f$-**sFDP** $\subset$ GaussDP
(Θ, ε)-aposteriori noiseless Pr [42]	B, F	$\checkmark^e$	$\checkmark^e$	?	(Θ, ε)-**ANPr** $\sim (\Theta, \varepsilon)$-NPr
(Θ, ε)-positive membership Pr [56]	B, F	$\checkmark^e$	$\checkmark^e$	$\boldsymbol{x}^h$	(Θ, ε)-**PMPr** $\supset \varepsilon$-BoDP

Table 10.5 (continued)

Name and References	Dimensions	Axioms		Composition	Relations
		Postprocessing	Convexity		
(Θ, ε)-negative membership Pr [56]	B, F	$\checkmark^e$	$\checkmark^e$	$\boldsymbol{\textit{✗}}^h$	(Θ, ε)-**NMPr** $\supset \varepsilon$-**BoDP**
(Θ, ε)-membership Pr [56]	B, F	$\checkmark^e$	$\checkmark^e$	$\boldsymbol{\textit{✗}}^h$	(Θ, ε)-**PMPr** $\prec (\Theta, \varepsilon)$-**MPr** $\succ (\Theta, \varepsilon)$-**NMPr**
$(\Theta, \varepsilon, \delta)$-adversarial Pr [57]	Q, B, F	$\checkmark^e$	$\checkmark^e$	$\boldsymbol{\textit{✗}}^h$	(ε, δ)-DP $\subset (\Theta, \varepsilon, \delta)$-**AdvPr** $\prec (\Theta, \varepsilon)$-**PMPr**
(Θ, ε)-information Pr [58]	N, B, F	?	?	?	(Θ, ε)-**InfPr** $\succ \varepsilon$-DP

^aSee Proposition 10.1.
^bSee Proposition 10.2.
^cSee Proposition 10.3.
^dSee Proposition 10.4.
^eSee Proposition 10.5.
^fSee Proposition 10.6.
^gSee Proposition 10.7.
^hSee Proposition 10.8.
ⁱFollows directly from its equivalence with ε-DP.
^jA proof appears in the paper introducing the definition.
^kA proof for a restricted scenario appears in the paper introducing the definition.
^lThis claim appears in [5], its proof is in the unpublished full version.

Table 10.6 Summary of DP modifications representing the main options in dimension R

Name and References	Dimensions	Axioms		Convexity	Composition	Relations
		Postprocessing				
$(\text{Agg}, \varepsilon)$-zero-knowledge Pr [59]	R	$\checkmark^j$		$\checkmark^j$	?[k]	$(\text{Agg}, \varepsilon)$-**ZKPr** $\succ \varepsilon$-DP
$(\mathcal{P}_v, \varepsilon, \delta)$-subspace DP [60]	Q, R	?[k]		?	$\checkmark^j$	$(\mathcal{P}_v, \varepsilon, \delta)$-SubDP $\prec(\varepsilon, \delta)$-DP
(P, ε)-bounded leakage DP [61]	Q, R	$\checkmark^j$		$\checkmark^j$	$\checkmark^j$	(P, ε)-**BLDP** $\supset(\varepsilon, \delta)$-DP
$(\Theta, \Gamma, \varepsilon)$-coupled-worlds Pr [62]	N, B, R	$\checkmark^j$		$\checkmark^j$	✗[c]	$(\Theta, \Gamma, \varepsilon)$-**CWPr** $\supset \varepsilon$-DP
$(\Theta, \Gamma, \varepsilon, \delta)$-inference CW Pr [62]	Q, N, B, F, R	?		?	✗[c]	$(\Theta, \Gamma, \varepsilon, \delta)$-**IBCWPr** $\succ(\Theta, \Gamma, \varepsilon)$-CWPr
$(\Theta, \Gamma, \varepsilon, \delta)$-inference DistDP [62]	Q, N, B, F, R	?		?	✗[c]	(Θ, ε)-DDP $\succ(\Theta, \Gamma, \varepsilon, \delta)$-**IBDDP** $\subset(\Theta, \Gamma, \varepsilon, \delta)$-IBCWPr
Typical Stability [63]	Q, V, R	?		?	✗[c]	$(\Theta, \gamma, \varepsilon, \delta)$-**TySt**

[a] See Proposition 10.1.
[b] See Proposition 10.2.
[c] See Proposition 10.3.
[d] See Proposition 10.4.
[e] See Proposition 10.5.
[f] See Proposition 10.6.
[g] See Proposition 10.7.
[h] See Proposition 10.8.
[i] Follows directly from its equivalence with ε-DP.
[j] A proof appears in the paper introducing the definition.
[k] A proof for a restricted scenario appears in the paper introducing the definition.
[l] This claim appears in [5], its proof is in the unpublished full version.

Table 10.7 Summary of DP modifications representing the main options in dimension C

Name and References	Dimensions	Axioms		Composition	Relations
		Postprocessing	Convexity		
ε_K-SIM-computational DP [64]	C	✓	✓	✓	ε_K-**SimCDP** $\prec\varepsilon$-DP
ε_K-IND-computational DP [64]	C	✓	✓	✓	ε_K-**IndCDP** $\prec\varepsilon_K$-SimCDP
(Agg, ε)-computational ZK Pr [59]	R, C	✓	✓	?	(Agg, ε)-**CZKPr** $\supset$ (Agg, ε)-ZKPr
(ε, δ, f)-output constrained DP [65]	N, V, C	✓	✓	✓	(ε, δ, f)-**OCDP** $\supset\varepsilon_K$-IndCDP
(ε, δ)-DP for record linkage [65]	N, V, C	✓	✓	✓	(ε, δ)-**RLDP** $\subset (\varepsilon, \delta, f)$-OCDP

a See Proposition 10.1.
b See Proposition 10.2.
c See Proposition 10.3.
d See Proposition 10.4.
e See Proposition 10.5.
f See Proposition 10.6.
g See Proposition 10.7.
h See Proposition 10.8.
i Follows directly from its equivalence with ε-DP.
j A proof appears in the paper introducing the definition.
k A proof for a restricted scenario appears in the paper introducing the definition.
l This claim appears in [5], its proof is in the unpublished full version.

Proposition 10.2 *ProDP and ACoDP do not satisfy the convexity axiom.*

Proof Consider the following mechanisms $\mathcal{M}_1$ and $\mathcal{M}_2$, with input and output in $\{0, 1\}$.

- $\mathcal{M}_1(0) = 0$, $\mathcal{M}_1(1) = 1$ with probability δ, and $\mathcal{M}_1(1) = 0$ with probability $1 - \delta$.
- $\mathcal{M}_2(0) = \mathcal{M}_2(1) = 1$.

Both mechanisms are $\left(\frac{1}{1-\delta}, \delta\right)$-ProDP. Now, consider the mechanism $\mathcal{M}$ which applies $\mathcal{M}_1$ with probability $1 - 2\delta$ and $\mathcal{M}_2$ with probability 2δ. $\mathcal{M}$ is a convex combination of $\mathcal{M}_1$ and $\mathcal{M}_2$, but the reader can verify that it is not $\left(\frac{1}{1-\delta}, \delta\right)$-ProDP. The result for (ξ, ρ, δ)-ACoDP is a direct corollary, since it is equivalent to (ξ, δ)-ProDP when $\rho = 0$.   □

Proposition 10.3 *$d_{\mathcal{D}}$-Pr satisfies both privacy axioms. Further, EDivDP also satisfies both privacy axioms.*

Proof The proof corresponding to PFPr in [45] is a proof by case analysis on every possible protected property. The fact that ε is the same for every protected property has no influence on the proof, so we can directly adapt the proof to $d_{\mathcal{D}}$-Pr and its combination with PFPr. Similarly, the proof can be extended to arbitrary divergence functions, like in Proposition 10.1.   □

Proposition 10.4 *RanDP does not satisfy the convexity axiom.*

Proof Let π be the uniform distribution on $\{0, 1\}$, let D_1 be generated by picking 10 records according to π, and D_2 by flipping one record at random. Let $\mathcal{M}_0$ return 0 if all records are 0, and $\perp$ otherwise. Let $\mathcal{M}_1$ return 1 if all records are 1, and $\perp$ otherwise.

Note that both mechanisms are $(\pi, 2^{-9}, 0)$-RanDP. Indeed, $\mathcal{M}_0$ will only return 0 for D_1 with probability 2^{-10}, and for D_2 with probability 2^{-10} (if D_1 only has one 1, which happens with probability $10 \cdot 2^{-10}$, and this record is flipped, which happens with probability 0.1). In both cases, $\mathcal{M}_0$ will return $\perp$ for the other database; which will be a distinguishing event. Otherwise, $\mathcal{M}_0$ will return τ for both databases, so $\mathcal{M}(D_1) \approx_0 \mathcal{M}(D_2)$. The reasoning is the same for $\mathcal{M}_1$.

However, the mechanism $\mathcal{M}_{0.5}$ obtained by applying either $\mathcal{M}_0$ or $\mathcal{M}_1$ uniformly randomly doesn't satisfy $(\pi, 2^{-9}, 0)$-RanDP: The indistinguishability property does not hold if D_1 or D_2 have all their records set to *either* 0 or 1, which happens twice as often as either option alone.   □

Proposition 10.5 *All variants of MPr, AdvPr, and ANPr satisfy both axioms. As a direct corollary, InfPr also satisfies both axioms.*

Proof We prove it for AdvPr. A mechanism $\mathcal{M}$ satisfies $(\Theta, \varepsilon, \delta)$-AdvPr if for all $t \in \mathcal{T}, \theta \in \Theta$, and $S \subseteq \mathcal{O}$, $\mathbb{P}_{D \sim \theta}[t \in D \mid \mathcal{M}(D) \in S] \leq e^{\varepsilon} \cdot \mathbb{P}_{D \sim \theta}[t \in D] + \delta$. We first prove that it satisfies the convexity axiom. Suppose $\mathcal{M}$ is a convex combination of $\mathcal{M}_1$ and $\mathcal{M}_2$. Simplifying $\mathbb{P}_{D \sim \theta}[\dots]$ into $\mathbb{P}[\dots]$, we have:

$$\mathbb{P}\left[t \in D \mid \mathcal{M}(D) \in S\right] = \frac{\mathbb{P}\left[t \in D \text{ and } \mathcal{M}(D) \in S \text{ and } \mathcal{M} = \mathcal{M}_1\right]}{\mathbb{P}\left[\mathcal{M}(D) \in S\right]}$$
$$+ \frac{\mathbb{P}\left[t \in D \text{ and } \mathcal{M}(D) \in S \text{ and } \mathcal{M} = \mathcal{M}_2\right]}{\mathbb{P}\left[\mathcal{M}(D) \in S\right]}$$

Denoting $X_i = \mathbb{P}\left[\mathcal{M}(D) \in S \text{ and } \mathcal{M} = \mathcal{M}_i\right]$ for $i \in \{1, 2\}$, this gives:

$$\mathbb{P}\left[t \in D \mid \mathcal{M}(D) \in S\right] = \frac{X_1 \cdot \mathbb{P}\left[t \in D \mid \mathcal{M}_1(D) \in S\right]}{X_1 + X_2}$$
$$\cdot \frac{X_2 \cdot \mathbb{P}\left[t \in D \mid \mathcal{M}_2(D) \in S\right]}{X_1 + X_2}$$
$$\leq \frac{X_1 \left(e^\varepsilon \cdot \mathbb{P}\left[t \in D\right]\right) + \delta}{X_1 + X_2} + \frac{X_2 \left(e^\varepsilon \cdot \mathbb{P}\left[t \in D\right]\right) + \delta}{X_1 + X_2}$$
$$\leq e^\varepsilon \cdot \mathbb{P}\left[t \in D\right] + \delta$$

The proof for the post-processing axiom is similar, summing over all possible outputs $\mathcal{M}(D)$. It is straightforward to adapt the proof to all other definitions which change the shape of the prior–posterior bounds. □

Proposition 10.6 *Both versions of CDP satisfy both privacy axioms; where the post-processing axiom is modified to only allow post-processing with functions computable on a probabilistic polynomial-time Turing machine. Consequently, CWPr and CZKPr also satisfies both privacy axioms.*

Proof For Ind-CDP and the post-processing axiom, the proof is straightforward: If post-processing, the output could break the ε-indistinguishability property, the attacker could do this on the original output and break the ε-indistinguishability property of the original definition.

For Ind-CDP and the convexity axiom, without loss of generality, we can assume that the sets of possible outputs of both mechanisms are disjoint (otherwise, this give strictly less information to the attacker). The proof is then the same as for the post-processing axiom.

For SimCDP, applying the same post-processing function to the "true" differentially private mechanism immediately leads to the result, since DP satisfies post-processing. The same reasoning holds for convexity. □

Composition

In this section, if $\mathcal{M}_1$ and $\mathcal{M}_2$ are two mechanisms, we denote $\mathcal{M}_{1+2}$ the mechanism defined by $\mathcal{M}_{1+2}(D) = (\mathcal{M}_1(D), \mathcal{M}_2(D))$.

Proposition 10.7 *If $\mathcal{M}_1$ is d_D^1-private and $\mathcal{M}_2$ is d_D^2-private, then $\mathcal{M}_{1+2}$ is d_D^{1+2}-private, where $d_D^{1+2}(D_1, D_2) = d_D^1(D_1, D_2) + d_D^2(D_1, D_2)$.*

Proof The proof is essentially the same as for ε-DP. $\mathcal{M}_1$'s randomness is independent from $\mathcal{M}_2$'s, so:

$$\mathbb{P}\begin{bmatrix} \mathcal{M}_1\,(D_1) = O_1\,\& \\ \mathcal{M}_2\,(D_1) = O_2 \end{bmatrix} = \mathbb{P}[\mathcal{M}_1\,(D_1) = O_1] \cdot \mathbb{P}[\mathcal{M}_2\,(D_1) = O_2]$$
$$\leq e^{d_{\mathcal{D}}^1(D_1,D_2)} \cdot \mathbb{P}[\mathcal{M}_2\,(D_2) = O_1] \cdot e^{d_{\mathcal{D}}^2(D_1,D_2)} \cdot \mathbb{P}[\mathcal{M}_2\,(D_2) = O_2]$$
$$\leq e^{d_{\mathcal{D}}^{1+2}(D_1,D_2)} \cdot \mathbb{P}[\mathcal{M}_1\,(D_2) = O_1 \text{and} \mathcal{M}_2\,(D_2) = O_2]$$

Most definition can also be combined with $d_{\mathcal{D}}$-privacy, and the composition proofs can be similarly adapted.   □

Proposition 10.8 *In general, definitions which assume limited background knowledge from the adversary do not compose.*

Proof The proof of Proposition 10.7 cannot be adapted to a context in which the attacker has limited background knowledge: As the randomness partially comes from the data-generating distribution, the two probabilities are no longer independent. A typical example considers two mechanisms which answer, e.g., queries "how many records satisfy property P" and "how many records satisfy property P and have an ID different from 4217": The randomness in the data might make each query private, but the combination of two queries trivially reveals something about a particular user. Variants of this proof can easily be obtained for all definitions with limited background knowledge.   □

References

1. Dwork, C., Kenthapadi, K., McSherry, F., Mironov, I., Naor, M.: Our data, ourselves: privacy via distributed noise generation. Springer, In Eurocrypt (2006)
2. Meiser, S.: Approximate and probabilistic differential privacy definitions. Cryptology ePrint Archive, Report 2018/277, 2018
3. Zhang, Z., Qin, Z., Zhu, L., Jiang, W., Xu, C., Ren, K.: Toward practical differential privacy in smart grid with capacity-limited rechargeable batteries (2015)
4. Cuff, P., Yu, L.: Differential privacy as a mutual information constraint. In: Proceedings of the 2016 ACM SIGSAC Conference on Computer and Communications Security. ACM (2016)
5. Mironov, I.: Renyi differential privacy. In: Computer Security Foundations Symposium (CSF), 2017 IEEE 30th. IEEE (2017)
6. Dwork, C., Rothblum, G.N.: Concentrated differential privacy. *arXiv preprint* arXiv:1603.01887 (2016)
7. Bun, M., Steinke, T.: Concentrated differential privacy: simplifications, extensions, and lower bounds. In: Theory of Cryptography Conference. Springer (2016)
8. Colisson, L.: L3 internship report: Quantum analog of differential privacy in term of rényi divergence (2016)
9. Bun, M., Dwork, C., Rothblum, G.N., Steinke, T.: Composable and versatile privacy via truncated cdp. In: Proceedings of the 50th Annual ACM SIGACT Symposium on Theory of Computing. ACM (2018)
10. Barber, R.F., Duchi, J.C.: Privacy and statistical risk: formalisms and minimax bounds. *arXiv preprint* arXiv:1412.4451 (2014)
11. Duchi, J.C., Ruan, F.: The right complexity measure in locally private estimation: it is not the fisher information. *arXiv preprint* arXiv:1806.05756 (2018)

12. Chaudhuri, K., Imola, J., Machanavajjhala, A.: Capacity bounded differential privacy. In: Advances in Neural Information Processing Systems (2019)
13. Kifer, D., Machanavajjhala, A.: No free lunch in data privacy. In: Proceedings of the 2011 ACM SIGMOD International Conference on Management of data. ACM (2011)
14. Kotsogiannis, I., Doudalis, S., Haney, S., Machanavajjhala, A., Mehrotra, S.: One-sided differential privacy. In: 2020 IEEE 36th International Conference on Data Engineering (ICDE), pp. 493–504. IEEE (2020)
15. Takagi, S., Cao, Y., Yoshikawa, M.: Asymmetric differential privacy. *arXiv preprint* arXiv:2103.00996 (2021)
16. Brendan McMahan, H., Ramage, D., Talwar, K., Zhang, L.: Learning differentially private recurrent language models. In: International Conference on Learning Representations (2018)
17. Asi, H., Duchi, J., Javidbakht, O.: Element level differential privacy: the right granularity of privacy. *arXiv preprint* arXiv:1912.04042 (2019)
18. Dwork, C.: Differential privacy: a survey of results. In: International Conference on Theory and Applications of Models of Computation. Springer (2008)
19. Liu, C., Chakraborty, S., Mittal, P.: Differential privacy under dependent tuples. In NDSS, Dependence makes you vulnberable (2016)
20. Yang, B., Sato, I., Nakagawa, H.: Bayesian differential privacy on correlated data. In: Proceedings of the 2015 ACM SIGMOD International Conference on Management of Data. ACM (2015)
21. Wu, X., Dou, W., Ni, Q.: Game theory based privacy preserving analysis in correlated data publication. In: Proceedings of the Australasian Computer Science Week Multiconference. ACM (2017)
22. Wu, X., Wu, T., Khan, M., Ni, Q., Dou, W.: Game theory based correlated privacy preserving analysis in big data. IEEE Trans. Big Data (2017)
23. Li, Y., Ren, X., Yang, S., Yang, X.: A unified analysis. IEEE Transactions on Information Forensics and Security, Impact of Prior Knowledge and Data Correlation on Privacy Leakage (2019)
24. Soria-Comas, J., Domingo-Ferrer, J., Sánchez, D., Megías, D.: Individual differential privacy: a utility-preserving formulation of differential privacy guarantees. IEEE Trans Inf For Secur (2017)
25. Redberg, R., Wang, Y.-X.: Privately publishable per-instance privacy. In: NeurIPS 2020 Competition and Demonstration Track. PMLR (2021)
26. Fang, C., Chang, E.-C.: Differential privacy with delta-neighbourhood for spatial and dynamic datasets. In: Proceedings of the 9th ACM Symposium on Information, Computer and Communications Security
27. Zhou, S., Ligett, K., Wasserman, L.: Differential privacy with compression. In: IEEE International Symposium on Information Theory, ISIT 2009, p. 2009. IEEE (2009)
28. Rubinstein, B.I.P., Aldà, F.: Pain-free random differential privacy with sensitivity sampling. In: Proceedings of the 34th International Conference on Machine Learning, vol. 70. JMLR.org (2017)
29. He, X., Machanavajjhala, A., Ding, B.: Blowfish privacy: tuning privacy-utility trade-offs using policies. In: Proceedings of the 2014 ACM SIGMOD International Conference on Management of Data. ACM (2014)
30. Jorgensen, Z., Yu, T., Cormode, G.: Conservative or liberal? Personalized differential privacy. In: 2015 IEEE 31st International Conference on Data Engineering (ICDE). IEEE (2015)
31. Lui, E., Pass, R.: Outlier privacy. In: Theory of Cryptography Conference. Springer (2015)
32. Gu, X., Li, M., Xiong, L., Cao, Y.: Providing input-discriminative protection for local differential privacy. In: 2020 IEEE 36th International Conference on Data Engineering (ICDE), pp. 505–516. IEEE (2020)
33. Hall, R., Wasserman, L., Rinaldo, A.: Random differential privacy. J. Privacy Confident. **4**(2) (2013)
34. Chatzikokolakis, K., Andrés, M.E., Bordenabe, N.E., Palamidessi, C.: Broadening the scope of differential privacy using metrics. In: International Symposium on Privacy Enhancing Technologies Symposium. Springer (2013)

35. Roth, A.: New algorithms for preserving differential privacy. Microsoft Research (2010)
36. Blum, A., Ligett, K., Roth, A.: A learning theory approach to noninteractive database privacy. J. ACM (JACM) (2013)
37. Triastcyn, A., Faltings, B.: Bayesian differential privacy for machine learning. In: International Conference on Machine Learning, pp. 9583–9592. PMLR (2020)
38. Wang, Y.-X., Lei, J., Fienberg, S.E.: On-average kl-privacy and its equivalence to generalization for max-entropy mechanisms. In: International Conference on Privacy in Statistical Databases. Springer (2016)
39. Dimitrakakis, C., Nelson, B., Mitrokotsa, A., Rubinstein, B., et al.: Bayesian differential privacy through posterior sampling. *arXiv preprint* arXiv:1306.1066 (2013)
40. Kawamoto, Y., Murakami, T.: Local distribution obfuscation via probability coupling. In: 2019 57th Annual Allerton Conference on Communication, Control, and Computing (Allerton). IEEE (2019)
41. Kifer, D., Lin, B.-R.: Towards an axiomatization of statistical privacy and utility. In: Proceedings of the Twenty-Ninth ACM SIGMOD-SIGACT-SIGART Symposium on Principles of Database Systems. ACM (2010)
42. Bhaskar, R., Bhowmick, A., Goyal, V., Laxman, S., Thakurta, A.: Noiseless database privacy. In: International Conference on the Theory and Application of Cryptology and Information Security. Springer (2011)
43. Desfontaines, D., Mohammadi, E., Krahmer, E., Basin, D.: Differential privacy with partial knowledge. *arXiv preprint* arXiv:1905.00650 (2019)
44. Li, N., Qardaji, W., Su, D.: On sampling, anonymization, and differential privacy or, k-anonymization meets differential privacy (2012)
45. Kifer, D., Machanavajjhala, A.: A rigorous and customizable framework for privacy. In: Proceedings of the 31st ACM SIGMOD-SIGACT-SIGAI Symposium on Principles of Database Systems. ACM (2012)
46. Leung, S., Lui, E.: Bayesian mechanism design with efficiency, privacy, and approximate truthfulness. In: International Workshop on Internet and Network Economics. Springer (2012)
47. Jelasity, M., Birman, K.P.: Distributional differential privacy for large-scale smart metering. In: Proceedings of the 2nd ACM Workshop on Information Hiding and Multimedia Security. ACM (2014)
48. Kawamoto, Y., Murakami, T.: Local obfuscation mechanisms for hiding probability distributions. In: European Symposium on Research in Computer Security. Springer (2019)
49. Geumlek, J., Chaudhuri, K.: Profile-based privacy for locally private computations. In: 2019 IEEE International Symposium on Information Theory (ISIT), pp. 537–541. IEEE (2019)
50. Liu, J., Xiong, L., Luo, J.: Semantic security: privacy definitions revisited. Trans. Data Privacy (2013)
51. Ganta, S.R., Kasiviswanathan, S.P., Smith, A.: Composition attacks and auxiliary information in data privacy. In: Proceedings of the 14th ACM SIGKDD International Conference on Knowledge Discovery and Data Mining. ACM (2008)
52. Kasiviswanathan, S.P., Smith, A.: On the 'semantics' of differential privacy: a Bayesian formulation. J. Privacy Confident. (2014)
53. Durfee, D., Rogers, R.M.: Practical differentially private top-k selection with pay-what-you-get composition. In: Advances in Neural Information Processing Systems (2019)
54. Dong, J., Roth, A., Su, W.: Gaussian differential privacy. J. R. Stat. Soci. (2021)
55. Zheng, Q., Chen, S., Long, Q., Su, W.: Federated f-differential privacy. In: International Conference on Artificial Intelligence and Statistics, pp. 2251–2259. PMLR (2021)
56. Li, N., Qardaji, W., Su, D., Wu, Y., Yang, W.: Membership privacy: a unifying framework for privacy definitions. In: Proceedings of the 2013 ACM SIGSAC Conference on Computer & Communications security. ACM (2013)
57. Rastogi, V., Hay, M., Miklau, G., Suciu, D.: Relationship privacy: output perturbation for queries with joins. In: Proceedings of the Twenty-Eighth ACM SIGMOD-SIGACT-SIGART symposium on Principles of Database Systems. ACM (2009)

58. du Pin Calmon, F., Fawaz,, N.: Privacy against statistical inference. In: 2012 50th Annual Allerton Conference on Communication, Control, and Computing (Allerton). IEEE (2012)
59. Gehrke, J., Lui, E., Pass, R.: Towards privacy for social networks: a zero-knowledge based definition of privacy. In: Theory of Cryptography Conference. Springer (2011)
60. Gao, J., Gong, R., Yu, F.-Y.: Subspace differential privacy. *arXiv preprint* arXiv:2108.11527 (2021)
61. Ligett, K., Peale, C., Reingold, O.: Bounded-leakage differential privacy. In: 1st Symposium on Foundations of Responsible Computing (FORC 2020). Schloss Dagstuhl-Leibniz-Zentrum für Informatik (2020)
62. Bassily, R., Groce, A., Katz, J., Smith, A.: Coupled-worlds privacy: exploiting adversarial uncertainty in statistical data privacy. In: 2013 IEEE 54th Annual Symposium on Foundations of Computer Science (FOCS). IEEE (2013)
63. Bassily, R., Freund, Y.: Typical stability. *arXiv preprint* arXiv:1604.03336 (2016)
64. Mironov, I., Pandey, O., Reingold, O., Vadhan, S.: Computational differential privacy. In: Advances in Cryptology-CRYPTO 2009. Springer (2009)
65. He, X., Machanavajjhala, A., Flynn, C., Srivastava, D.: Composing differential privacy and secure computation: a case study on scaling private record linkage. In: Proceedings of the 2017 ACM SIGSAC Conference on Computer and Communications Security. ACM (2017)

Chapter 11
Scope and Related Work

In this chapter, we detail our criteria for excluding particular data privacy definitions from our book, we list some relevant definitions that were excluded by this criteria, and we list related works and existing surveys in the field of data privacy.

11.1 Methodology

Whether a data privacy definition fits our description is not always obvious, so we use the following criterion: The attacker's capabilities must be clearly defined, and the definition must prevent this attacker from learning about a protected property. Consequently, we do not consider:

- definitions which are a property of the output data and not of the mechanism,
- variants of technical notions that are not data privacy properties, like the different types of sensitivity;
- definitions whose only difference with DP is in the context and not in the formal property, like the distinction between local and global models.

In Sect. 11.2, we give a list of notions that we found during our survey and considered to be out of scope for our book. To find a comprehensive list of DP notions, besides the definitions we were aware of or were suggested to us by experts, we conducted a wide literature review using two research datasets: BASE[1] and Google Scholar.[2] The exact queries were run several times: November 1st in 2018, August 1st in 2019, June 1st in 2020, and 1st of September in 2021. The final result count are summarized in Table 11.1.

---

[1] https://www.base-search.net/.

[2] https://scholar.google.com/.

© The Author(s), under exclusive license to Springer Nature Switzerland AG 2022
B. Pejó and D. Desfontaines, *Guide to Differential Privacy Modifications*,
SpringerBriefs in Computer Science,
https://doi.org/10.1007/978-3-030-96398-9_11

Table 11.1 Queries for the literature review

Query (BASE)	Hits
"Differential privacy" relax	194
"Differential privacy" variant-relax	225
Query (Google Scholar)	Hits
"Differential privacy" "new notion"	332
"Differential privacy" "new definition"—"new notion"	248

First, we manually reviewed each paper and filtered them out until we had only papers which contained either a new definition or were applying DP in a new setting. All papers which defined a variant or extension of DP are cited in this book.

11.2   Out of Scope Definitions

As detailed in the previous section, we considered certain data privacy definitions to be out of scope for our book, even when they seem to be related to differential privacy. This section elaborates on such definitions.

Lack of semantic guarantees

Some definitions do not provide clear semantic privacy guarantees or are only used as a tool in order to prove links between existing definitions. As such, we did not include them in our survey.

- ε-*privacy*,[3] introduced in [1], was a first attempt at formalizing an adversary with restricted background knowledge by using Dirichlet distribution. This definition imposes a condition on the output, but not on the mechanism, consequently it does not offer strong semantic guarantees like noiseless privacy [2, 3] (introduced in Chap. 6).
- *Relaxed indistinguishability*, introduced in [4] is a relaxation of adversarial privacy that provides a plausible deniability by requiring for each tuple, that at least l tuples must exist with ε-indistinguishability. However, it does not provide any guarantee against Bayesian adversaries.
- *Mutual-information DP*, introduced in [5] is an alternative way to average the privacy loss, similar to Chap. 3. It formalize the intuition that any individual record should not "give out too much information" on the output of the mechanism (or vice versa).
- *Individual privacy*, introduce in [6] is also a mutual-information-based extension of DP which can encapsulate the (deterministic) secure multiparty com-

---

[3] Another definition with the same name is introduced later in this section.

putations [7]; hence, we exclude it due to the lack of clear semantic privacy guarantees.

- *Differential identifiability*, introduced in [8], bounds the probability that a given individual's information is included in the input datasets but does not measure the "change" in probabilities between the two alternatives. As such, it does not provide any guarantee against Bayesian adversaries.[4]
- *Crowd-blending privacy*, introduced in [10], combines differential privacy with k-anonymity. As it is strictly weaker than any mechanism which always returns a k-anonymous dataset, the guarantees it provides against a Bayesian adversary are unclear. It is mainly used to show that combining crowd-blending privacy with pre-sampling implies zero-knowledge privacy [10, 11].
- (k, ε)-*anonymity*, introduced in [12], first performs k-anonymization on a subset of the quasi-identifiers and then ε-DP on the remaining quasi-identifiers with different settings for each equivalence class of the k-anonymous dataset. The semantic guarantees of this definition are not made explicit.
- *Integral privacy*, introduced in [13] looks at the inverse of the mechanism $\mathcal{M}$, and require all outputs O to be generated by a large and diverse set of databases D. This could capture definitions like k-anonymity, but offer no semantic guarantee in the Bayesian sense.
- *Membership privacy*,[5] introduced in [14] is tailored to membership inference attacks on machine learning models; the guarantees it provides are not clear.
- *Posteriori DP*, introduced in [15], compares two posteriors in a way similar to inferential privacy in Chap. 7, but does not make the prior (and thus, the attacker model) explicit.
- ε-*privacy*,[6] introduced in [16], adopts DP to location data and protect only the secret locations, but it only offers absolute bounds irrespectively of the prior.
- *Noiseless privacy*,[7] and *measure of privacy*, introduced in [17, 18] limits the change in the number of possible outputs when one record in the dataset changes and determines privacy using non-stochastic information theory, respectively. Consequently, they do not bound the change in "probabilities" of the mechanism, so do not seem to offer clear guarantees against a Bayesian adversary.
- *Weak DP*, introduced in [19], adapts DP for streams, but it only provides a DP guarantee for the "average" of all possible mechanism outputs,[8] rather than for the mechanism itself. Thus, its semantics guarantees are also unclear.
- *Data privacy* and *multi-dimensional data privacy*, introduce in [20, 21], ensures that an attacker's inference accuracy and disclosure probability is below some thresholds.

---

[4] Although it was reformulated in [9] as an instance of membership privacy introduced in Chap. 7.

[5] Another definition with the same name is introduced in [9], we mention it in Chap. 7.

[6] Another definition with the same name is introduced earlier in this section.

[7] Another definition with the same name is introduced in [2, 3], we mention it in Sect. 6.

[8] It also assumes that some uncertainty comes from the data itself, similarly to definitions in Sect. 7.

- *Error Preserving Privacy*, introduced in [22], states that the "variance" of the adversary's error when trying to guess a given user's record does not change significantly after. The exact adversary model is not specified.

Variants of sensitivity

A important technical tool used when designing differentially private mechanisms is the "sensitivity" of the function that we try to compute. There are many variants to the initial concept of global sensitivity [23], including local sensitivity [24], smooth sensitivity [24], restricted sensitivity [25], empirical sensitivity [26], empirical differential privacy[9][10] [29], recommendation-aware sensitivity [30], record and correlated sensitivity [31], dependence sensitivity [32], per-instance sensitivity [33], individual sensitivity [34], elastic sensitivity [35], distortion sensitivity [36], and derivative and partial sensitivity [37, 38], respectively. We did not consider these notions as these do not modify the actual definition of differential privacy.

11.3 Local Model and Other Contexts

In this book, we focused on DP modifications typically used in the "global model," in which a central entity has access to the whole dataset. It is also possible to use DP in other contexts, without formally changing the definition. The main alternative is the "local model," where each individual randomizes their own data before sending it to an aggregator. This model is surveyed in [39] and formally introduced in [40].

Many definitions we listed were initially presented in the local model, such as $d_\mathcal{D}$-privacy [41], geo-indistinguishability [42], earth mover's Pr [43], location Pr [44], profile-based DP [45], input-discriminative DP [46], divergence DP and smooth DP from [47], and extended DP, distribution Pr, and extended distribution Pr from [48]. Below, we list the definitions that are the same as previously listed definitions, but used in a different attacker setting; the list also includes alternatives to the local and global models.

- In [49], the authors introduce *distributed DP*, which corresponds to local DP, with the additional assumption that only a portion of participants are honest.
- In [50], the authors define *joint DP*, to model a game in which each player cannot learn the data from any other player, but are still allowed to observe the influence of their data on the mechanism output.
- In [51], authors define a slightly different versions of joined DP, called *multiparty DP*, in which the view of each "subgroup" of players is differentially private with respect to other players inputs.
- In [52], the authors define *DP in the shuffled model*, which falls in-between the global and the local model: the local model is augmented by an anonymous channel

---

[9] Even though it is introduced as a variant of DP, it was later shown to be a measure of sensitivity [27].

[10] Another definition with the same name is introduced in [28], we mention it in Chap. 6.

that randomly permutes a set of user-supplied messages, and differential privacy is only required of the output of the shuffler.

- In [53], the authors defined *local DP for bandits*, a local version of *instantaneous DP* (mentioned in Chap. 4).
- In [54], the authors define *task-global DP* and *task-local DP*, which are equivalents of element-level DP (mentioned in Chapter 4) in a meta-learning context.
- In [55], the authors define *utility-optimized local DP*, a local version of one-sided differential privacy (mentioned in Chap. 4) which additionally guarantees that if the data is considered sensitive, then a certain set of outputs is forbidden.
- In [56–59], the authors define *personalized local DP*, a local version of personalized DP (mentioned in Chap. 5).
- In [60], the authors define $d_{\mathcal{D}}$-*local DP*, a local version of $d_{\mathcal{D}}$-DP (mentioned in Chap. 5); this was defined as *condensed local DP* in [61].
- In [62], the authors define *localized information privacy*, a local version of information privacy (mentioned in Chap. 7).

11.4 Related Work

Some of the earliest surveys focusing on DP summarize algorithms achieving DP and applications [63, 64]. The more detailed "privacy book" [65] presents an in-depth discussion about the fundamentals of DP, techniques for achieving it, and applications to query-release mechanisms, distributed computations, or data streams. Other recent surveys [66, 67] focus on the release of histograms and synthetic data with DP and describing existing privacy metrics and patterns while providing an overall view of different mathematical privacy-preserving framework.

In [68], the authors classify different privacy enhancing technologies (PETs) into seven complementary dimensions. Indistinguishability falls into the "Aim" dimension, but within this category, only k-anonymity and oblivious transfer are considered; differential privacy is not mentioned. In [69], the authors survey privacy concerns, measurements, and privacy-preserving techniques used in online social networks and recommender systems. They classify privacy into five categories: DP falls into "Privacy-preserving models" along with, e.g., k-anonymity. In [70], the authors classified 80+ privacy metrics into 8 categories based on the output of the privacy mechanism. One of their classes is "Indistinguishability," which contains DP as well as several variants. Some variants are classified into other categories; for example, Rényi DP is classified into "Uncertainty" and mutual-information DP into *Information gain/loss*. The authors list eight differential privacy variants; our taxonomy can be seen as an extension of the contents of their work (and in particular of the "Indistinguishability" category).

In [15], authors establish connections between differential privacy (seen as the additional disclosure of an individual's information due to the release of the data), "identifiability" (seen as the posteriors of recovering the original data from the released data) and "mutual-information privacy" (which measures the average amount of information about the original dataset contained in the released data).

The relation between the main syntactic models of anonymity and DP was studied in [71], in which the authors claim that the former is designed for privacy-preserving data publishing (PPDP), while DP is more suitable for privacy-preserving data mining (PPDM). The survey [72] investigates the issue of privacy loss due to data correlation under DP models and classifies existing literature into three categories: using parameters to describe data correlation, using models to describe data correlation, and describing data correlation based on the framework.

Other surveys focus on location privacy. In [73], the authors highlight privacy concerns in this context and list mechanisms with formal provable privacy guarantees; they describe several variants of differential privacy for streaming (e.g., pan-privacy) and location data (e.g., geo-indistinguishability) along with extensions such as pufferfish and blowfish privacy. In [74], the authors analyze different kinds of privacy breaches and compare metrics that have been proposed to protect location data.

Finally, the appropriate selection of the privacy parameters for DP was also exhaustively studied. This problem in not trivial, and many factors can be considered: In [75], the authors used economic incentives, in [76–78], the authors looked at individual preferences, and in [79, 80], the authors took into account an adversary's capability in terms of hypothesis testing and guessing advantage, respectively.

References

1. Machanavajjhala, A., Gehrke, J., Götz, M.: Data publishing against realistic adversaries. In: Proceedings of the VLDB Endowment (2009)
2. Duan, Y.: Privacy without noise. In: Proceedings of the 18th ACM Conference on Information and Knowledge Management. ACM (2009)
3. Bhaskar, R., Bhowmick, A., Goyal, V., Laxman, S., Thakurta, A.: Noiseless database privacy. In: International Conference on the Theory and Application of Cryptology and Information Security. Springer (2011)
4. Rastogi, V., Hay, M., Miklau, G., Suciu, D.: Relationship privacy: output perturbation for queries with joins. In: Proceedings of the Twenty-Eighth ACM SIGMOD-SIGACT-SIGART Symposium on Principles of Database Systems. ACM (2009)
5. Cuff, P., Yu, L.: Differential privacy as a mutual information constraint. In: Proceedings of the 2016 ACM SIGSAC Conference on Computer and Communications Security. ACM (2016)
6. Li, Q., Gundersen, J.S., Heusdens, R., Christensen, M.G.: Privacy-preserving distributed processing: metrics, bounds and algorithms. IEEE Trans. Inf. For. Secur. **16**, 2090–2103 (2021)
7. Goldwasser, S., Micali, S.: Probabilistic encryption. J. Comput. Syst. Sci. (1984)
8. Lee, J., Clifton, C.: Differential identifiability. In: Proceedings of the 18th ACM SIGKDD International Conference on Knowledge Discovery and Data Mining. ACM (2012)
9. Li, N., Qardaji, W., Su, D., Wu, Y., Yang, W.: Membership privacy: a unifying framework for privacy definitions. In: Proceedings of the 2013 ACM SIGSAC Conference on Computer & Communications Security. ACM (2013)
10. Gehrke, J., Hay, M., Lui, E., Pass, R.: Crowd-blending privacy. In: Advances in Cryptology– CRYPTO 2012. Springer (2012)
11. Lui, E., Pass, R.: Outlier privacy. In: Theory of Cryptography Conference. Springer (2015)

12. Holohan, N., Antonatos, S., Braghin, S., Mac Aonghusa, P.: (k,e)-anonymity: k-anonymity with e-differential privacy. *arXiv preprint* arXiv:1710.01615
13. ç Torra, V., Navarro-Arribas, G.: Integral privacy. In: International Conference on Cryptology and Network Security, pp. 661–669. Springer (2016)
14. Sablayrolles, A., Douze, M., Schmid, C., Ollivier, Y., Jégou, H.: White-box vs black-box: Bayes optimal strategies for membership inference. In: International Conference on Machine Learning, pp. 5558–5567. PMLR (2019)
15. Wang, W., Ying, L., Zhang, J.: On the relation between identifiability, differential privacy, and mutual-information privacy. IEEE Trans. Inf. Theory (2016)
16. Partovi, A., Zheng, W., Jung, T., Lin, H.: Ensuring privacy in location-based services: a model-based approach. *arXiv preprint* arXiv:2002.10055
17. Farokhi, F.: Noiseless privacy: Definition, guarantees, and applications. IEEE Trans. Big Data (2021)
18. Farokhi, F.: Development and analysis of deterministic privacy-preserving policies using non-stochastic information theory. IEEE Trans Inf For Secur **14**(10), 2567–2576 (2019)
19. Wang, Y., Sibai, H., Mitra, S., Dullerud, G.E.: Differential privacy for sequential algorithms. *arXiv preprint* arXiv:2004.00275
20. He, J., Cai, L., Guan, X.: Preserving data-privacy with added noises: optimal estimation and privacy analysis. IEEE Trans. Inf. Theory **64**(8), 5677–5690 (2018)
21. Sun, M., Zhao, C., He, J., Cheng, P., Quevedo, D.: Privacy-preserving correlated data publication: privacy analysis and optimal noise design. IEEE Trans. Netw. Sci. Eng. (2020)
22. Nguyen, T.D.: Gupta, S., Rana, S., Venkatesh, S.: A privacy preserving bayesian optimization with high efficiency. In: Pacific-Asia Conference on Knowledge Discovery and Data Mining. Springer (2018)
23. Dwork, C., McSherry, F., Nissim, K., Smith, A.: Calibrating noise to sensitivity in private data analysis. In: Theory of Cryptography Conference. Springer (2006)
24. Nissim, K., Raskhodnikova, S., Smith, A.: Smooth sensitivity and sampling in private data analysis. In: Proceedings of the Thirty-Ninth Annual ACM Symposium on Theory of Computing. ACM (2007)
25. Blocki, J., Blum, A., Datta, A., Sheffet, O.: Differentially private data analysis of social networks via restricted sensitivity. In: Proceedings of the 4th Conference on Innovations in Theoretical Computer Science. ACM (2013)
26. Chen, S., Zhou, S.: Recursive mechanism: towards node differential privacy and unrestricted joins. In: Proceedings of the 2013 ACM SIGMOD International Conference on Management of Data. ACM (2013)
27. Charest, A.-S., Hou, Y.: On the meaning and limits of empirical differential privacy. J. Privacy Confident. (2016)
28. Burchard, P., Daoud, A.: Empirical differential privacy. *arXiv preprint* arXiv:1910.12820
29. Abowd, J.M., Schneider, M.J., Vilhuber, L.: Differential privacy applications to Bayesian and linear mixed model estimation. J. Privacy Confident. (2013)
30. Zhu, T., Li, G., Ren, Y., Zhou, W., Xiong, P.: Differential privacy for neighborhood-based collaborative filtering. In: Proceedings of the 2013 IEEE/ACM International Conference on Advances in Social Networks Analysis and Mining. ACM (2013)
31. Zhu, T., Xiong, P., Li, G., Zhou, W.: Correlated differential privacy: hiding information in non-iid data set. IEEE Trans. Inf. For. Secur. (2015)
32. Liu, C., Chakraborty, S., Mittal, P.: Differential privacy under dependent tuples. In: NDSS, Dependence Makes You Vulnberable (2016)
33. Redberg, R., Wang, Y.-X.: Privately publishable per-instance privacy. In: NeurIPS 2020 Competition and Demonstration Track. PMLR (2021)
34. Cummings, R., Durfee, D.: Individual sensitivity preprocessing for data privacy. In: Proceedings of the Fourteenth Annual ACM-SIAM Symposium on Discrete Algorithms. SIAM (2020)
35. Johnson, N., Near, J.P., Song, D.: Towards practical differential privacy for sql queries. In: Proceedings of the VLDB Endowment (2018)

36. Bansal, A., Chunduru, R., Data, D., Prabhakaran, M.: Robustness and Flexibility, Extending the Foundations of Differential Privacy (2019)
37. Laud, P., Pankova, A., Martin, P.: Achieving differential privacy using methods from calculus. *arXiv preprint* arXiv:1811.06343
38. Mueller, T.T., Ziller, A., Usynin, D., Knolle, M., Jungmann, F., Rueckert, D., Kaissis, G.: Partial sensitivity analysis in differential privacy. *arXiv preprint* arXiv:2109.10582
39. Yang, M., Lyu, L., Zhao, J., Zhu, T., Lam, K.-Y.: Local differential privacy and its applications: a comprehensive survey. *arXiv preprint* arXiv:2008.03686
40. Duchi, J.C., Jordan, M.I., Wainwright, M.J.: Local privacy and statistical minimax rates. In: 2013 IEEE 54th Annual Symposium on Foundations of Computer Science (FOCS). IEEE (2013)
41. Chatzikokolakis, K., Andrés, M.E., Bordenabe, N.E., Palamidessi, C.: Broadening the scope of differential privacy using metrics. In: International Symposium on Privacy Enhancing Technologies Symposium. Springer (2013)
42. Andrés, M.E., Bordenabe, N.E., Chatzikokolakis, K., Palamidessi, C.: Geo-indistinguishability: differential privacy for location-based systems. In: Proceedings of the 2013 ACM SIGSAC Conference on Computer & Communications Security. ACM (2013)
43. Fernandes, N., Dras, M., McIver, A.: Generalised differential privacy for text document processing. In: International Conference on Principles of Security and Trust. Springer (2019)
44. ElSalamouny, E., Gambs, S.: Differential privacy models for location-based services. Trans. Data Privacy (2016)
45. Geumlek, J., Chaudhuri, K.: Profile-based privacy for locally private computations. In: 2019 IEEE International Symposium on Information Theory (ISIT), pp. 537–541. IEEE (2019)
46. Gu, X., Li, M., Xiong, L., Cao, Y.: Providing input-discriminative protection for local differential privacy. In: 2020 IEEE 36th International Conference on Data Engineering (ICDE), pp. 505–516. IEEE (2020)
47. Barber, R.F., Duchi, J.C.: Privacy and statistical risk: formalisms and minimax bounds. *arXiv preprint* arXiv:1412.4451
48. Kawamoto, Y., Murakami, T.: Local obfuscation mechanisms for hiding probability distributions. In: European Symposium on Research in Computer Security. Springer (2019)
49. Shi, E., Chan, H.T.H., Rieffel, E., Chow, R., Song, D.: Privacy-preserving aggregation of time-series data. In: Annual Network & Distributed System Security Symposium (NDSS). Internet Society (2011)
50. Kearns, M., Pai, M., Roth, A., Ullman, J.: Mechanism design in large games: incentives and privacy. In: Proceedings of the 5th Conference on Innovations in Theoretical Computer Science. ACM (2014)
51. Wu, G., He, Y., Wu, J., Xia, X.: Inherit differential privacy in distributed setting: multiparty randomized function computation. In: Trustcom/BigDataSE/I SPA, 2016 IEEE. IEEE (2016)
52. Bittau, A., Erlingsson, Ú., Maniatis, P., Mironov, I., Raghunathan, A., Lie, D., Rudominer, M., Kode, U., Tinnes, J., Seefeld, B.: Prochlo: strong privacy for analytics in the crowd. In: Proceedings of the 26th Symposium on Operating Systems Principles. ACM (2017)
53. Basu, D., Dimitrakakis, C., Tossou, A.: Differential privacy for multi-armed bandits: What is it and what is its cost? *arXiv preprint* arXiv:1905.12298
54. Li, J., Khodak, M., Caldas, S., Talwalkar, A.: Differentially private meta-learning. In: International Conference on Learning Representations (2019)
55. Murakami, T., Kawamoto, Y.: Utility-optimized local differential privacy mechanisms for distribution estimation. In: 28th USENIX Security Symposium (USENIX Security 19) (2019)
56. Dobbe, R., Pu, Y., Zhu, J., Ramchandran, K., Tomlin, C.: Customized local differential privacy for multi-agent distributed optimization. *arXiv preprint* arXiv:1806.06035
57. Nie, Y., Yang, W., Huang, L., Xie, X., Zhao, Z., Wang, S.: A utility-optimized framework for personalized private histogram estimation. IEEE Trans. Knowl. Data Eng. (2018)
58. Acharya, J., Bonawitz, K., Kairouz, P., Ramage, D., Sun, Z.: Context aware local differential privacy. In: International Conference on Machine Learning, pp. 52–62. PMLR (2020)

59. Shen, Z., Xia, Z., Yu, P.: Pldp: Personalized local differential privacy for multidimensional data aggregation. Secur. Commun. Netw. **2021** (2021)
60. Alvim, M., Chatzikokolakis, K., Palamidessi, C., Pazii, A.: Local differential privacy on metric spaces: optimizing the trade-off with utility. In: 2018 IEEE 31st Computer Security Foundations Symposium (CSF). IEEE (2018)
61. Gursoy, M.E., Tamersoy, A., Truex, S., Wei, W., Liu, L.: Secure and utility-aware data collection with condensed local differential privacy. IEEE Trans. Depend. Secur. Comput. (2019)
62. Jiang, B., Li, M., Tandon, R.: Context-aware data aggregation with localized information privacy. In: 2018 IEEE Conference on Communications and Network Security (CNS), pp. 1–9. IEEE (2018)
63. Dwork, C.: Differential privacy: a survey of results. In: International Conference on Theory and Applications of Models of Computation. Springer (2008)
64. Dwork, C.: The differential privacy frontier. In: Theory of Cryptography Conference. Springer (2009)
65. Dwork, C., Roth, A., et al.: The algorithmic foundations of differential privacy. In: Foundations and Trends® in Theoretical Computer Science (2014)
66. Nelson, B., Reuben, J.: Sok: Chasing accuracy and privacy, and catching both in differentially private histogram publication. *arXiv* (2019)
67. Rajendran, S., Prabhu, J.: A novel study of different privacy frameworks metrics and patterns. In: Advances in Distributed Computing and Machine Learning, pp. 181–196. Springer (2021)
68. Heurix, J., Zimmermann, P., Neubauer, T., Fenz, S.: A taxonomy for privacy enhancing technologies. Comput. Secur. (2015)
69. Aghasian, E., Garg, S., Montgomery, J.: User's privacy in recommendation systems applying online social network data, a survey and taxonomy. *arXiv preprint* arXiv:1806.07629
70. Wagner, I., Eckhoff, D.: Technical privacy metrics: a systematic survey. ACM Comput. Surv. (CSUR) (2018)
71. Clifton, C., Tassa, T.: On syntactic anonymity and differential privacy. In: 2013 IEEE 29th International Conference on Data Engineering Workshops (ICDEW). IEEE (2013)
72. Zhang, T., Zhu, T., Liu, R., Zhou, W.: Correlated data in differential privacy: definition and analysis. In: Concurrency and Computation: Practice and Experience, p. e6015 (2020)
73. Machanavajjhala, A., He, X.: Analyzing your location data with provable privacy guarantees. In: Handbook of Mobile Data Privacy. Springer (2018)
74. Chatzikokolakis, K., ElSalamouny, E., Palamidessi, C., Anna, P., et al.: Methods for location privacy: a comparative overview. Found. Trends® Privacy Secur. (2017)
75. Hsu, J., Gaboardi, M., Haeberlen, A., Khanna, S., Narayan, A., Pierce, B.C., Roth, A.: Differential privacy: an economic method for choosing epsilon. In: 2014 IEEE 27th Computer Security Foundations Symposium. IEEE (2014)
76. Lee, J., Clifton, C.: How much is enough? choosing ε for differential privacy. In: International Conference on Information Security. Springer (2011)
77. Krehbiel, S.: Choosing epsilon for privacy as a service. In: Proceedings on Privacy Enhancing Technologies (2019)
78. Pejo, B., Tang, Q., Biczók, G.: Together or alone: the price of privacy in collaborative learning. In: Proceedings on Privacy Enhancing Technologies (2019)
79. Liu, C., He, X., Chanyaswad, T., Wang, S., Mittal, P.: Investigating statistical privacy frameworks from the perspective of hypothesis testing. In: Proceedings on Privacy Enhancing Technologies (2019)
80. Laud, P., Pankova, A.: Interpreting epsilon of differential privacy in terms of advantage in guessing or approximating sensitive attributes. *arXiv preprint* arXiv:1911.12777

Chapter 12
Conclusion

We proposed a classification of differential privacy modifications using the concept of dimensions. When possible, we compared definitions from the same dimension, and we showed that definitions from the different dimensions can be combined to form new, meaningful definitions. In theory, it means that even if there were only three possible ways to change a dimension (e.g., making it weaker or stronger or leaving it as is), this would result in $3^7 = 2187$ possible definitions: The 200 semantically different already existing definitions shown in Fig. 1.1 are only scratching the surface of the space of possible notions.

Using these dimensions, we unified and simplified the different notions proposed in the literature. We highlighted their properties such as composability and whether they satisfy the privacy axioms by either collecting the existing results or creating new proofs, and whenever possible, we showed their relative relations to one another. We hope that this book will make the field of data privacy more organized and easier to navigate in.

© The Author(s), under exclusive license to Springer Nature Switzerland AG 2022
B. Pejó and D. Desfontaines, *Guide to Differential Privacy Modifications*,
SpringerBriefs in Computer Science,
https://doi.org/10.1007/978-3-030-96398-9_12

Printed in the United States
by Baker & Taylor Publisher Services